Learning Language Arts Through Literature

THE GREEN

TEACHER BOOK

By

Diane Welch and Susan Simpson

Common Sense Press

The *Learning Language Arts Through Literature* Series:

The Blue Book - 1st Grade Skills
The Red Book - 2nd Grade Skills
The Yellow Book - 3rd Grade Skills
The Orange Book - 4th Grade Skills
The Purple Book - 5th Grade Skills
The Tan Book - 6th Grade Skills
The Green Book - 7th-8th Grade Skills
The Gray Book - 8th-9th Grade Skills
The Gold Book - High School Skills

Scripture taken from the
NEW AMERICAN STANDARD BIBLE®
©Copyright The Lockman Foundation
1960,1962,1963,1968,1971,1972,1973,1975,1977
Used by Permission

Copyright ©1998 by:

Common Sense Press
8786 Highway 21
P.O. Box 1365
Melrose, FL 32666
(352) 475-5757
Website: http://www.cspress.com

All rights reserved. No part of this book may be reproduced in any form without written permission from Common Sense Press.

Printed in the United States of America.

ISBN 1-880892-34-0

Introduction

As parents we watched and marveled at the way our little ones learned to talk. By listening and responding to English spoken well, they were able to communicate quite clearly. The process was so gradual that they were not even aware it was taking place.

It is the belief of those associated with the *Learning Language Arts Through Literature* series that written language can best be learned in the same manner. By reading fine literature and working with good models of writing, children will receive a quality education in language arts. If you desire to teach using this integrated approach to language, this curriculum is for you.

In her books, Dr. Ruth Beechick has confirmed that this method of teaching is an appropriate and successful way to introduce our students to the joys of reading, writing, and thinking. Our own experiences using these lessons with children have encouraged us to share them with you. Their enjoyment and enthusiasm for reading and writing is an unmatched recommendation for this method of teaching.

The **integrated language approach** has the benfits of all teaching methods. By working with pieces of literature, you focus on grammar, vocabulary, writing, reading, spelling, penmanship, and thinking skills. Your student has the best advantage for learning skills in this effective and lasting manner.

Grammar is taught in conjunction with writing, not as much as an isolated subject. Your student's **vocabulary** will be enhanced by reading the good literature which has been carefully chosen for his grade level. We realize that every student functions at reading different levels. For the more hesitant reader, we recommend, you, the teacher read aloud with your student. Grade appropriate **reading skills** are included. Helpful **Spelling Tips** are included to help your student develop his spelling skills. **Penmanship** skills may be developed as your student writes his dictation or any other writing assignment. Handwriting is influenced by maturity of fine motor ability so the goal is to improve from the point at which your student begins. **Thinking skills** are developed throughout the activities in this manual. Anytime a student is asked to respond to the literature with discussion, writing, drawing, or completing an activity, your student is developing higher order thinking skills.

How to Use This book

The Green Book is divided into eleven sections:

Everyday Words (thirteen weeks) - The twelve dictation lessons in this unit will provide a thorough review of the parts of sentences. As a further re-enforcement the student will learn how to diagram the parts in order to strengthen his understanding of how these parts fit together. This unit has been divided into five smaller units and distributed throughout the book, enabling the student to enjoy a variety of activities in between.

Since your dictation passages are taken from books that you would enjoy reading, the sentences are more complex than the easy-reading books you enjoyed when you were younger. This means that the sentence parts might not be as easily recognized. In order for you to practice recognizing these basic parts, you will be given three options.

1. You may analyze sentences in easy-reading books you have at home or check out from the library.

2. You may write sentences illustrating the parts indicated.

3. You may copy or take from dictation the sentences provided for you.

Poetry Unit (six weeks) - The student will develop an appreciation for poetry while memorizing, reciting, and analyzing the works of different poets. In addition, he will be writing his own poems and a psalm. A dictation lesson is provided later in the book as a review.

Book Study on *Star of Light* (three weeks) - While reading this book the student will complete such assignments as writing character sketches, comparing and contrasting cultures and religions, drawing maps, narrating, and more.

The Short Story Unit (three weeks) - The student will enjoy exploring the elements of the short story. He will be able to develop a story line, write dialogue, identify the conflict of a story as well as its climax and resolution.

Book Study on *Adam and His Kin* (four weeks) - A narrative history of the first eleven chapters of Genesis by Dr. Ruth Beechick is the basis for this four-week unit. The student will develop skills in researching, drawing graphs, and writing narration.

Book Study on the Play *Much Ado About Nothing* (three weeks) - The student will read and study a Shakespearean play, developing the ability to understand and enjoy the work of this great playwright.

Research Unit (four weeks) - The student will learn the research process in manageable steps. These include choosing a topic, taking notes, formulating an outline, writing a first draft, making revisions, completing the final draft, and writing a bibliography.

Review Activites
Review Activities are found directly after each *Everyday Words*. New skills taught in each lesson are included in the *Review Activities*. It is not necessary to do each activity. Choose the skills your student needs.

Assessments
Following each *Everyday Words* section, you will find an assessment.

Skills Index
The *Language Arts Skills Index* is located in the back of the manual. To ensure that skills commonly held appropriate for seventh and eighth grade instruction were adequately covered, much research was involved in the writing of this book.

Enrichment Activities
At the end of the lessons and units you will find the treasure chest icon for the *Enrichment Activities*. This is your cue to look for the activity located in the *Student Activity Book* where they are listed in full. Use these activities as needed throughout the lesson or unit. Answers to these activities are found at the end of this manual. While optional, these activities develop thinking and reasoning skills necessary for higher level learning.

Bibliography

Next you will find the *Bibliography*. This will give you all the information you need to locate the books quoted in the lessons. The selection includes wonderful books that we hope your family will read and enjoy.

Materials To Use

To use the manual you will need pencils, paper, colored pencils, drawing paper, a notebook, file folders, and construction paper. Additional materials are listed at the beginning of each lesson. Frequently in the lessons, the student must find a book he is familiar with, so children's books or other easy-reading books are needed from time to time.

Previous lessons are often used again, so keep all the student's work until the entire unit is completed.

Reference books, such as dictionary and thesaurus, will be used as well as encyclopedias. Availability of these materials in either the home or library is adequate.

Student Activity Books

Student Activity Books are available for your student. Daily exercises corresponding to each lesson are included for easy use.

Table of Contents

Squire Gordon's Park skirted the village of Birtwick. It was entered by a large iron gate, at which stood the first lodge, and then you trotted along on a smooth road between clumps of large old trees; then another lodge and another gate which brought you to the house and the gardens. Beyond this lay the home paddock, the old orchard, and the stables. There was accommodation for many horses and carriages, but I need only describe the stable into which I was taken. This was very roomy, with four good stalls. A large swinging window opened into the yard, which made it pleasant and airy.

Black Beauty by Anna Sewell

Black Beauty
by Anna Sewell
Several publications are
available for your choice.

✏ **Teacher's Note: As your student completes this lesson, choose skills from the *Review Activties* that he needs. The *Review Activities* follow this lesson.**

1. a. Take the literature passage from dictation. Proofread, looking for any spelling or punctuation errors.

   b. Make a spelling list to study this week or use the following suggested list: lodge, trotted, accommodation, carriages.

   If a word has a soft **/g/** sound following a single short vowel, the **/g/** sound is often spelled **dge**.

> ### Spelling Tip
> Words with a soft **/g/** sound preceded by a single short vowel will often be spelled with **dge.**

Write the following words, and underline **dge.** Say the words aloud as you write them.

lodge	dodge	ledge
fudge	badger	ridge
midget	fridge	

Anna Sewell (1820-1878) was born into a strict Quaker home where she was educated by her mother and father. At the age of 14, she was injured in a fall and left a cripple for the rest of her life. During the final days of her illness, she was confined to her home and began to write *Black Beauty*, her only book. Her reason for writing the book: "Perhaps it might make men a little kinder to their faithful horses." *Black Beauty* was published in 1877, and Anna lived just long enough to hear of its success.

2. a. Look at this word: *enter.*
The word *enter* is called a **base** or **root word**. Sometimes a letter or a group of letters is added to a word.

Look at this word: *entered.*
The letters **-ed** has been added to the end of the base word. This is called a suffix. A **suffix** is a letter or a group of letters added to the end of a base or root word. The suffix will often tell you what part of speech the word is.
Ex: music - noun
    musical - adjective
    musician - noun
    musically - adverb

b. Before you add a suffix beginning with a vowel, like **-ed**, look at the word. If the word ends with one vowel and one consonant, double the consonant before you add the suffix.

Spelling Tip
Words like **trot** which end with one vowel and one consonant need a double consonant before adding a suffix beginning with a vowel.

c. Add the suffix **-ed** and **-ing** to the following words. Say the words aloud as you write them.

	-ed	**-ing**
Ex: trot	trot**ted**	trot**ting**

1) stop
2) pat
3) clap
4) jog

2. c.
1) stopped stopping
2) patted patting
3) clapped clapping
4) jogged jogging

d. God has created us with a need to communicate with one another. Writing and speaking are the most common forms of communication and both depend upon words. When we combine words into meaningful patterns we are able to communicate. To make sure we are expressing our thoughts clearly we must learn how to write good sentences and punctuate them properly.

A **complete sentence** expresses a complete thought and is made up of two main parts: a subject and a predicate. The **complete subject** is the part which tells who or what the sentence is about. The **complete predicate** is the part that tells something about the subject.

e. Read the first sentence in the literature passage. The sentence is about *Squire Gordon's Park. Squire Gordon's Park* is the complete subject.

Underline the complete subject in each of the following sentences. Remember, the complete subject tells who or what the sentence is about.
Ex: <u>The stable</u> was roomy.

1) A tall broad man stepped forward.
2) The master backed me a little.
3) My new master was an unmarried man.
4) My feet slipped from under me.
5) We stopped at the hotel.

f. What does the first sentence in the literature passage tell you about *Squire Gordon's Park*?

This is called the complete predicate. The complete predicate tells something about the subject. Predicate means *to proclaim or tell*.

g. Look at the sentences you worked with in **2e**. Draw a vertical line after the complete subject. Everything to the right of the line is the complete predicate.
Ex: The stable / was roomy.

2.
e.1) <u>A tall broad man</u> stepped forward.
   2) <u>The master</u> backed me a little.
   3) <u>My new master</u> was an unmarried man.
   4) <u>My feet</u> slipped from under me.
   5) <u>We</u> stopped at the hotel.

f. It tells that it *skirted the village of Birtwick.*

g.
   1) A tall broad man / stepped forward.
   2) The master / backed me a little.
   3) My new master / was an unmarried man.
   4) My feet / slipped from under me.
   5) We / stopped at the hotel.

h. Practice dividing sentences between the complete subject and complete predicate in your easy-reading books. (See Introduction.)

OR

i. Write your own sentences and divide.

OR

j. Use the following sentences, and draw a vertical line to separate the complete subject and complete predicate.
Ex: The frightened dog / ran away.

1) The bright stars twinkled above.
2) A single rose was still on the bush.
3) The boy laughed loudly.
4) Her eyes snapped angrily.
5) The day is clear and bright.

3. a. The complete subject will always contain a noun or pronoun. A **noun** is a person, place, thing, or idea. *Boy, state, cup,* and *love* are examples of **common nouns**. *Robert* names a particular boy and *Arkansas* names a particular state. These words are called **proper nouns**. Proper nouns always begin with a **capital letter**. (Pronouns will be discussed in **3e**.)

Ex: planet - Jupiter (name of a particular planet)
    girl - Sandra (name of a particular girl)
    day of the week - Tuesday (name of a particular day)

Note: Capitalize the months, but not the seasons.

b. Write a proper noun for the following common nouns.
1) month
2) country
3) woman
4) dog
5) city

c. Look at the following sentence.

The young boy / jumped for joy.

2.
j. 1) The bright stars /
   twinkled above.
   2) A single rose / was still
   on the bush.
   3) The boy / laughed
   loudly.
   4) Her eyes / snapped
   angrily.
   5) The day / is clear and
   bright.

3.
b. Possible Answers:
   1) February
   2) Japan
   3) Sandra Dumas
   4) Ruff
   5) Charleston

The left side of the sentence is called the complete subject. What is the main word in the complete subject which names a person, place, thing, or idea? *Boy* is the simple subject. The **simple subject** will always be a noun or pronoun without any describing words.

d. Underline the simple subject in the following sentences.
Ex: The <u>stable</u> / was roomy.

1) A tall broad man / stepped forward.
2) The master / backed me a little.
3) My new master / was an unmarried man.
4) My feet / slipped from under me.

e. Look at the following sentence.

We / stopped at the hotel.

There is only one word in the complete subject of this sentence. Underline it. This is a pronoun. A **pronoun** is a word which takes the place of a noun. Look at the Personal Pronoun Chart.

3.
d.1) A tall broad <u>man</u> / stepped forward.
2) The <u>master</u> / backed me a little.
3) My new <u>master</u> / was an unmarried man.
4) My <u>feet</u> / slipped from under me.

e. <u>We</u>

PERSONAL PRONOUNS		
Singular		
Subjective	**Possessive**	**Objective**
1st person　　I	my, mine	me
2nd person　you	your, yours	you
3rd person　she/ he/ it	her/ hers/ his/ its	her/ him/ it
Plural		
Subjective	**Possessive**	**Objective**
1st person　we	our, ours	us
2nd person　you	your, yours	you
3rd person　they	their, theirs	them

3.
f. It, you, you, I, I, it

4.
b. <u>skirted</u>

d.
1) A tall broad man
<u>stepped</u> forward. (AV)
2) The master <u>backed</u> me a
little. (AV)
3) My new master <u>was</u> an
unmarried man. (BV)
4) My feet <u>slipped</u> from
under me. (AV)
5) We <u>stopped</u> at the hotel.
(AV)

---

f. List the personal pronouns found in the literature passage.

g. Review your spelling words.

4. a. Just as the complete subject contains a simple subject, the complete predicate contains a simple predicate. The simple predicate is called the **verb**. The verb gives the sentence meaning by telling us something about the subject. A verb expresses action or a state of being. When a verb shows what a person or thing does, it is called an **action verb**. Action verbs are words such as *run, laugh,* or *trust.*   A simple way of finding the action verb is to see if the verb sounds right in the following blanks:

> He _____s. He is _____ing.
> Ex: He wanders.   He is wandering.

b. Using this exercise, underline the action verb twice in the first sentence of the literature passage.

c. When a verb shows what a person or thing is being, it is called a **being verb**.

Being Verbs			
am	is	are	was
were	be	being	been

d. Look at the following sentences. Underline the verb twice in each sentence. Write if they are action verbs (**AV**) or being verbs (**BV**).

1) A tall broad man stepped forward.
2) The master backed me a little.
3) My new master was an unmarried man.
4) My feet slipped from under me.
5) We stopped at the hotel.

e. Underline the simple subject once and underline the verb twice in the following sentences. Write if they are action (**AV**) or being verbs (**BV**).

   1) The bright stars twinkled above.
   2) A single red rose was still on the bush.
   3) The boy laughed loudly.
   4) Her eyes snapped angrily.
   5) The day is clear and bright.

f. Optional: Take an oral or written spelling pretest.

5. a. Take the literature passage from dictation again.
                              OR
   b. Practice finding the complete subject and complete predicate in your easy-reading books. Then find the simple subject and verb for those sentences. Is the verb action or being?
                              OR
   c. Write five sentences dividing between the complete subject and complete predicate. Underline the simple subject once and underline the verb twice. Is the verb action or being?
                              OR
   d. Choose skills from the *Review Activities* on the next page.

e.
1) The bright <u>stars</u> <u>twinkled</u> above. (AV)
2) A single red <u>rose</u> <u>was</u> still on the bush.(BV)
3) The <u>boy</u> <u>laughed</u> loudly. (AV)
4) Her <u>eyes</u> <u>snapped</u> angrily. (AV)
5) The <u>day</u> <u>is</u> clear and bright. (BV)

Review Activities

Choose the skills your student needs to review.

1. *Complete Subject / Complete Predicate*
   Separate the sentences with a vertical line between the complete subject and complete predicate. Underline the simple subject once and underline the verb twice. Write if they are action verbs (**AV**) or being verbs (**BV**).

   a. The silvery moon shone brightly.
   b. My favorite hobby is coin collecting.
   c. Red lights flashed.
   d. I laughed at my own mistakes.
   e. The raging river devastated the village.
   f. The small cat hissed at the strange dog.
   g. My bicycle is red.
   h. The girl kicked the ball.
   i. His mother turned off the light.
   j. A loud noise pierced the night.

2. *Common and Proper Nouns / Capitalization*
   Write the following sentences replacing the underlined words with a proper noun.

   a. The boy rafted down the river.
   b. Neal went to Richmond with the boys.
   c. The children will be in the play.
   d. I hope the girls remember their lines.
   e. The boys played volleyball.

3. *Pronouns*
   Replace the bolded words with the correct pronoun.

   a. Bill treated **Steve and Adam** to an ice cream cone.
   b. **Steve and Adam** thanked Bill.
   c. Adam borrowed **Steve's** bicycle.
   d. **Bill and I** ate dinner outside.
   e. Bill went to **Steve and Adam's** house.

4. *Verbs - Action and Being*
   Write a sentence using a being verb.
   Write a sentence using an action verb.

1.
a. The silvery <u>moon</u> / <u>shone</u> brightly. (AV)
b. My favorite <u>hobby</u> / <u>is</u> coin collecting. (BV)
c. Red <u>lights</u> / <u>flashed</u>. (AV)
d. <u>I</u> / <u>laughed</u> at my own mistakes. (AV)
e. The raging <u>river</u> / <u>devastated</u> the village.(AV)
f. The small <u>cat</u> / <u>hissed</u> at the strange dog. (AV)
g. My <u>bicycle</u> / <u>is</u> red. (BV)
h. The <u>girl</u> / <u>kicked</u> the ball. (AV)
i. His <u>mother</u> / <u>turned</u> off the light. (AV)
j. A loud <u>noise</u> / <u>pierced</u> the night. (AV)

2. Possible answers:
a. Nathan
b. Carl and Brian
c. Jennifer and Bob
d. Alice and Melissa
e. Ben and Sam

3.
a. them
b. They
c. his
d. we
e. their

4.
a. Answers will vary.
b. Answers will vary.

John seemed very proud of me. He used to make my mane and tail almost as smooth as a lady's hair, and he would talk to me a great deal. Of course, I did not understand all he said, but I learned more and more to know what he <u>meant</u>, and what he wanted me to do. I grew very fond of him. He was so gentle and kind. He seemed to know the tender places, and the ticklish places. When he brushed my head, he went as carefully over my eyes as if they were his own, and never stirred up any ill-temper.

Black Beauty by Anna Sewell

1. a. Take the literature passage from dictation. Proofread, looking for any spelling or punctuation errors.

   b. Make a spelling list to study this week or use the following suggested list: gentle, carefully, stirred, understand.

   Before adding the suffix **-ful** to a word, look at the word. If the word ends with a consonant and **y**, change **y** to **i** and add **-ful.** If the word ends with a vowel and **y,** just add **-ful.** If the word ends with any other letter, just add **-ful.**

   Note: Remember that the suffix **-ful** is spelled with only one **l.**

> ### Spelling Tip
> When adding **-ful** to a word
> ending with a consonant and **y,**
> change the **y** to **i** before adding **-ful,**
> otherwise just add **-ful.**

✏ **Teacher's Note: As your student completes this lesson, choose skills from the *Review Activties* that he needs. The *Review Activities* follow this lesson.**

1. c.
1) plentiful   plentifully
2) bountiful   bountifully
3) wonderful   wonderfully
4) colorful   colorfully
5) joyful   joyfully

d. A pronoun is a word that takes the place of a noun.

e. John seemed very proud of *Black Beauty*. *John* used to make *Black Beauty's* mane and tail almost as smooth as a lady's hair, and *John* would talk to *Black Beauty* a great deal. Of course, *Black Beauty* did not understand all *John* said, but *Black Beauty* learned more and more to know what *John* meant, and what *John* wanted *Black Beauty* to do. *Black Beauty* grew very fond of *John*. *John* was so gentle and kind. *John* seemed to know the tender places, and the ticklish places. When *John* brushed *Black Beauty's* head, *John* went as carefully over *Black Beauty's* eyes as if *Black Beauty's* eyes were *John's* own, and never stirred up any ill-temper.

c. Add the suffix. Say the words aloud as you write them.

	-ful	-fully
Ex: car**e**	care**ful**	care**fully**
Ex: pl**ay**	play**ful**	play**fully**
Ex: beau**ty**	beaut**iful**	beaut**ifully**

1) plenty
2) bounty
3) wonder
4) color
5) joy

d. In Lesson 1, you learned about pronouns. Do you remember the definition of a pronoun?

e. The noun that a pronoun replaces is called the **antecedent**. Without pronouns, the literature passage would be very awkward to read. Read the passage substituting the appropriate antecedent for the pronouns used.
Ex: John seemed very proud of *Black Beauty*. *John* used to make *Black Beauty's* mane...

2. a. As you learned in Lesson 1, sentences can be divided into two main parts - the complete subject and the complete predicate. The complete subject will always have a noun or pronoun as the simple subject. The complete predicate will always contain a verb.

Read the following sentence:

John did seem very proud of me.

John is the subject. The verb is *did seem*. A verb may consist of more than one verb. This is called a verb phrase. A **verb phrase** contains one main verb and one or more **helping verbs**. Sometimes a verb phrase may be separated by another word.
Ex: Jim *has* not *left*.

The following are some common helping verbs. Being verbs may also be used as helping verbs. It will help you to memorize these.

Common Helping Verbs				
have	has	had	do	does
did	shall	will	should	would
may	might	must	can	could

Being Verbs		
am	is	
are	were	was
be	being	been

b. Underline the verbs twice in the following sentences. Some sentences may contain a verb phrase. Circle the helping verbs.

1) John brushed my hair.
2) He had made it like a lady's hair.
3) He would talk to me a great deal.
4) John had spoken kindly to me.

c. Using the sentences in **2b**, box all the pronouns.

d. Using the same sentences above, list all the nouns. Beside each noun, write if it is a common noun (**CN**) or proper noun (**PN**).

3. a. Look at the second sentence in the literature passage. Why do you think *lady's hair* is written with an apostrophe **s** (**'s**)?

   For a noun to show possession, you must add an apostrophe **s** (**'s**). This is called a **singular possessive noun**.

b. Complete the following by making possessive nouns.
   Ex: hair belonging to the lady - lady**'s** hair

   1) mane belonging to the horse
   2) eyes belonging to the man
   3) book belonging to John

2.
b. 1) John <u>brushed</u> my hair.
   2) He (had) <u>made</u> it like a lady's hair.
   3) He (would) <u>talk</u> to me a great deal.
   4) John (had) <u>spoken</u> kindly to me.

c.
1) my
2) He, it
3) He, me
4) me

d.
1) John - (PN) ; hair - (CN)
2) hair - (CN)
3) deal - (CN)
4) John - (PN)

3.
a. To show that the hair belonged to the lady

b. 1) horse's mane
   2) man's eyes
   3) John's book

3.
c. 1) teachers' desks
**   2) animals' food**

d. 1) mice's hole
**   2) men's jackets**
**   3) women's cars**

f. 1) Sir Issac Newton
**   2) Jonathon Kimble, Jr.**
**   3) Dr. J. T. Scott**

c. To make a possessive noun of plural words ending with **s**, usually just add an apostrophe ('). This is called a **plural possessive noun**.

Complete the following by making plural possessive nouns.
Ex: the room belonging to the boys - boys' room

1) desks belonging to the teachers
2) food belonging to the animals

Some nouns form their plural by changing completely. These words are **irregular** and form their plural possessive by adding an apostrophe **s** (**'s**).
Ex: the dog belonging to more than one child - children**'s** dog

d. Complete the following by making plural possesive nouns.
1) the hole belonging to more than one mouse
2) the jackets belonging to more than one man
3) the cars belonging to more than one woman

e. In Lesson 1, you learned to capitalize all proper nouns such as names of people, countries, days of the week, etc. Also capitalize the **titles of people** which come before or after the name. Capitalize initials and punctuate with a **period** after **abbreviations** and **initials**. If the title comes after the name, add a comma after the name.
Ex: Mr. John Chang
     Dr. Selma Dugan
     Mrs. T.M. Lindberg
     Samuel Kowalski, Esq.
     (Notice the comma when the title comes after the name.)

f. Capitalize and punctuate the following.
1) sir issac newton
2) jonathan kimble jr
3) dr j t scott

g. When writing the **title of a book**, capitalize the first word and every other important word. If the title is handwritten, underline it. If it is computer generated, use italics.

h. Capitalize and underline the following titles of books.
    Ex: <u>Last of the Mohicans</u> - handwritten
         Last of the Mohicans - computer generated

     1) the adventures of huckleberry finn
     2) all creatures great and small
     3) where the lilies bloom

i. You have learned to capitalize proper nouns. When referring to proper nouns of more than one word, capitalize each important word.
    Ex: Amazon River
         Mount Everest
         Red Sea
         Lakeside Community Church
         Rawlings & Company

j. Capitalize the proper nouns.
    1) yellow river
    2) lake superior
    3) caspian sea
    4) civil war
    5) united states of america

k. Review your spelling words.

4. a. Today, you will begin learning how to diagram the basic parts of a sentence. There are several reasons why learning to diagram sentences will be beneficial to you.

First, for those of you who enjoy puzzles, diagramming sentences will make learning sentence parts more enjoyable. Second, while diagramming sentences is not done by anyone on a regular basis, it is an ability that educated people have acquired. Lastly, the visual analysis of a sentence will be helpful in learning a second language. Although the sentence structure may vary for this new language, a clear understanding of terminology and a concept of the parts of speech in our language will help you comprehend the grammar of the new language.

3.

h.
1) <u>**The Adventures of Huckleberry Finn**</u> - handwritten
The Adventures of Huckleberry Finn - computer generated
2) <u>**All Creatures Great and Small**</u> - handwritten
All Creatures Great and Small - computer generated
3) <u>**Where The Lilies Bloom**</u> - handwritten
Where The Lilies Bloom - computer generated

j. 1) Yellow River
    2) Lake Superior
    3) Caspian Sea
    4) Civil War
    5) United States of America

Note: For the next few lessons, the words which are to be diagrammed will always be bolded. You will eventually learn how to diagram complete sentences.

Since the foundation of a sentence is the simple subject and the simple predicate (verb), we will always start diagramming sentences with these two parts as follows:

subject | verb

Note: *Always* diagram the helping verbs with the verb.

From henceforth, the simple subject and simple predicate will be referred to as the subject and verb.

b. Diagram only the subject and verb of the following sentences. The subject and verb are bolded.

1) A tall broad **man stepped** forward.
2) The **master backed** me a little.
3) My new **master was** an unmarried man.
4) My **feet slipped** from under me.
5) **We stopped** at the principal hotel.

c. Diagram only the subject and verb in these sentences. The subject and verb are bolded.

1) **John seemed** very proud of me.
2) **I grew** very fond of him.
3) **He was** so gentle and kind.

d. Optional: Take an oral or written spelling pretest.

5. a. Take the literature passage from dictation.
                    OR
   b. Locate and diagram only the subject and verb of sentences in your easy-readers.
                    OR
   c. Write your own sentences and then diagram the subject and verb.
                    OR
   d. Choose skills from the *Review Activities* on the next page. If you are not sure about a sentence in your easy-readers, skip it and go on to another. Some questions will be cleared up in future lessons.

4.
b. 1) ___man| stepped___
   2) master| backed
   3) master| was
   4) ___feet |slipped___
   5) ___We |stopped___

c. 1) __John| seemed__
   2) ___I |grew___
   3) __He | was__

Review Activities

Choose the skills your student needs to review.

1. *Antecedent*
   Circle the pronouns. Write the words to which the pronouns refer.

   a. Heather lost her wallet.
   b. Carl looked for her wallet but couldn't find it.
   c. Heather asked her mother if she saw it.
   d. Terry and Lynn found it at their house.
   e. Heather thanked them.

2. *Verb Phrase / Helping Verbs*
   Underline the verb phrase and circle the helping verb.

   a. Chris has been waiting a long time.
   b. He did not know you left.
   c. I am reading a book.
   d. You could have come with me.
   e. Jeremy has been sleeping all night.

3. *Possessive Nouns / Singular and Plural*
   Write the correct possessive noun.

   a. kayak belonging to the boys
   b. lunchroom belonging to the teachers
   c. the bicycle belonging to the child
   d. the umbrella belonging to Jane
   e. the garden belonging to Jenny

4. *Capitalization / Punctuation (Titles of people, titles of books, abbreviations, initials)*
   Capitalize and punctuate the following.

   a. swiss family robinson (title of a book)
   b. around the world in eighty days (title of a book)
   c. robert williams jr
   d. mr thomas riveras
   e. dr jd lang

1.
a. her - Heather
b. her - Heather; it - wallet
c. her - Heather; she - mother; it - wallet
d. it - wallet; their - Jerry and Lynn
e. them - Jerry and Lynn

2.
a. Chris (has)(been) waiting a long time.
b. He (did) not know you left.
c. I (am) reading a book.
d. You (could)(have) come with me.
e. Jeremy (has)(been) sleeping all night.

3.
a. boys' kayak
b. teachers' lunchroom
c. child's bike
d. Jane's umbrella
e. Jenny's garden

4.
a. <u>Swiss Family Robinson</u> or *Swiss Family Robinson*
b. <u>Around the World in Eighty Days</u> or *Around the World in Eighty Days*
c. Robert Williams, Jr.
d. Mr. Thomas Riveras
e. Dr. J.D. Lang

5.
a. Rocky Mountains
b. Red Sea
c. Columbia River
d. South Carolina
e. Pacific Ocean

6.

a.   John | ran

b.   I | will finish

c.   clouds | covered

d.   weatherman | predicted

e.   I | could see

f.   stars | twinkled

g.   rose | was

h.   boy | laughed

i.   eyes | snapped

j.   day | is

5. *Proper Nouns / Capitalization*
Capitalize the proper nouns.

   a. rocky mountains
   b. red sea
   c. columbia river
   d. south carolina
   e. pacific ocean

6. *Diagram / Subject and Verb*
Diagram only the subject and verb. The subject and the verb have been bolded.

   a. **John ran** home.
   b. Tomorrow, **I will finish** my project.
   c. Dark **clouds covered** the sky.
   d. The **weatherman predicted** snow for tomorrow.
   e. On top of the mountain, **I could see** the entire city.
   f. The bright **stars twinkled** above.
   g. A single **rose was** still on the bush.
   h. The **boy laughed** loudly.
   i. Her **eyes snapped** angrily.
   j. The **day is** clear and bright.

> *The perfect rest, the good food, the soft turf, and gentle exercise soon began to tell on my condition and my spirits. I had a good constitution from my mother, and I was never strained when I was young, so that I had a better chance than many horses, who have been worked before they came to their full strength. During the winter my legs improved so much that I began to feel quite young again.*

Black Beauty by Anna Sewell

Teacher's Note: As your student completes this lesson, choose skills from the *Review Activties* that he needs. The *Review Activities* follow this lesson.

1. a. Take the literature passage from dictation. Proofread, looking for any spelling or punctuation errors.

   b. Make a spelling list to study this week or use the following suggested list: perfect, exercise, condition, strength.

   Words with the **/shun/** sound are usually spelled **-tion** or **-sion**. Words are rarely spelled **-shun**.

   > ### Spelling Tip
   > Words with the **/shun/** sound are usually spelled **-tion** or **-sion**.

   c. Write the following words, and underline the suffixes **-tion** and **-sion**. Say the words aloud as you write them.

-tion	**-sion**
condition	permission
mention	submission
vacation	admission
section	aversion
relation	depression
nation	tension
collection	session

d. How did you do with the punctuation in the dictation? Look at the first sentence of the literature passage. **Commas** are used to separate words or groups of words used in a series. *The perfect rest, the good food, the soft turf, and gentle exercise* are separated by commas.

The comma is used to separate words.
Ex: The celebration was unique, fun, and exciting.

The comma is used to separate phrases.
Ex: We are going to hike the trails, set up camp, and sleep under the stars.

e. Add commas to the following sentences.

1) Sheryl sliced some apples oranges and bananas.
2) Don planted the seeds Mary watered them and the family enjoyed the harvest.

f. Write a sentence naming at least three things. Remember the commas.

g. There are several meanings for the word *constitution*. Look up the word in the dictionary. Remember to use the guide words at the top of the page to help you find a word quickly. **Guide words** tell you the first and last words listed on each page. What is the meaning of the word *constitution* as used in this paragraph?

2. a. The first sentence of the literature passage tells you that Black Beauty experienced rest.

1) What kind of rest?
2) What kind of food?
3) What kind of turf?
4) What kind of exercise?

These words are called adjectives. An **adjective** is a word that modifies (changes the meaning of something in such a way as to limit it or make it more specific) a noun or pronoun.

Note: *Her, the, a, an, Jerry's* are special adjectives and will be covered in **2e**.

---

1. e.
1) Sheryl sliced some apples, oranges, and bananas.
2) Don planted the seeds, Mary watered them, and the family enjoyed the harvest.

f. Answers will vary.

g. principles

✎ **Teacher's Note:**
Dictionaries vary in how guide words are used. Refer to your dictionary and teach this skill accordingly.

2.
a. 1) perfect rest
** 2) good food**
** 3) soft turf**
** 4) gentle exercise**

Adjectives answer the following questions:
  What kind?
  How many?
  Which one?
  Whose?

I am sure you have looked through the lens of a camera or a microscope. At first glance, what you see is blurry, but you adjust the lens and bring it into focus. This is what adjectives do for us. For example, the word *dog* doesn't bring a distinct picture to our minds. But if we read *small dog*, the picture becomes a little clearer. If we read *small, black, scruffy dog* the picture is sharper yet. While the subject and verb are the foundation of a sentence, the adjectives (or modifiers) help make the meaning of the sentence clearer and more interesting.

b. Look at the following sentences about *Black Beauty*. Underline the adjectives, and draw an arrow to the noun it describes. Write the question they answer.
  What kind?
  How many?
  Which one?
  Whose?

Ex: Several men boarded the train. how many

1) Her long, beautiful hair was streaming behind her back.
2) The sad day had come.
3) Three weeks had passed after the conversation.
4) An old gentleman was riding with him.

c. Look again at this sentence:

Her long, beautiful hair was streaming behind her back.

What separates the adjectives *long* and *beautiful*?

Use a **comma** to separate two or more adjectives.

2.
b.1) Her long, beautiful hair was streaming behind her back. what kind

2) The sad day had come. what kind

3) Three weeks had passed after the conversation. how many

4) An old gentleman was riding with him. what kind

c. a comma

2.

d.1) The man crept up the old, squeaky stairs.

2) I met a kind, elderly woman.

3) Heavy, dark clouds covered the sky.

f.

1) [Her] **long, beautiful hair was streaming behind** [her] **back.**

2) (The) **sad day had come.**

3) (A) **droll smile came over** Jerry's **face.**

4) Three weeks had passed after (the) **conversation.**

5) (An) **old gentleman was riding with** [his] **wife.**

d. Add commas to the following sentences as needed.

1) The man crept up the old squeaky stairs.
2) I met a kind elderly woman.
3) Heavy dark clouds covered the sky.

e. In addition to the adjectives we have studied, there are three special types of adjectives that we use more than any others:

- Articles - *a, an, the*
- Possessive nouns - words like *Joe's, boy's, cats', men's*
- Possessive pronouns - *my, mine, your(s), his, her(s), its, our(s), their(s)*

f. Circle the articles in the following sentences. Draw a box around the possessive pronouns. Underline the possessive nouns.

1) Her long, beautiful hair was streaming behind her back.
2) The sad day had come.
3) A droll smile came over Jerry's face.
4) Three weeks had passed after the conversation.
5) An old gentleman was riding with his wife.

3. a. In the first sentence of the literature passage, the *turf* is said to be *soft*. If we were to compare it to another turf we could say it was *softer* than the other turf. If we compared it to several different turfs, we could say it was the *softest* turf.

Most adjectives can be compared using the suffix **-er** when comparing two things. This is called the **comparative form**. Use the suffix **-est** when comparing three or more things. This is called the **superlative form**. Most three or more syllable words use the words *more* or *most* to show comparisons.

Ex: clean - cleaner - cleanest
excellent - more excellent - most excellent

Be careful. Some one-syllable words use *more* or *most*. Some adjectives may form their comparative and superlative either way.

Ex: fun - more fun - most fun

Write the comparative and superlative forms for the adjectives you found yesterday in **2b**.

Note: Some adjectives will not have a comparative or superlative form.

Positive	**Comparative**	**Superlative**
Ex: small	small**er**	small**est**
Ex: brilliant	more brilliant	most brilliant

1) long
2) beautiful
3) sad
4) old

Three does not have a comparative or superlative form.

b. Write sentences using the comparative and superlative forms for three of the listed words.

c. Review your spelling words.

4. a. Adjectives are diagrammed on an angled line attached to the base line below the word modified. If there is more than one adjective, add another line.

Note: Always diagram articles, possessive pronouns, and possessive nouns as adjectives.

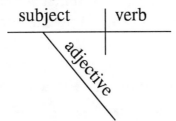

b. Diagram only the subject, verb, and adjective in the following sentences. Words to be diagramed are bolded.
Ex: **Her long, beautiful hair was streaming** behind her.

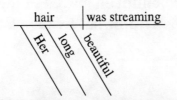

3. a.
	Comparitive	Superlative
1)	longer	longest
2)	more beautiful	
		most beautiful
3)	sadder	saddest
4)	older	oldest

b. Answers will vary.

21

4.
b.

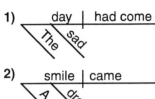

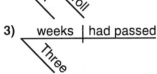

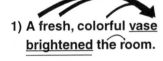

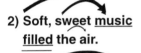

4.d&e.

1) A fresh, colorful <u>vase</u> <u>brightened</u> the room.

2) Soft, sweet <u>music</u> <u>filled</u> the air.

3) Five hungry <u>children</u> <u>stared</u> at me.
no comma

4) A shiny, crisp <u>apple</u> <u>sat</u> by his plate.

f.

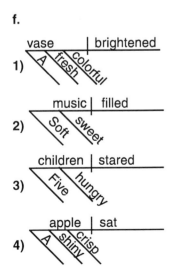

1) **The sad day had come**.
2) **A droll smile came** over Jerry's face.
3) **Three weeks had passed** after the conversation.
4) **An old gentleman was riding** with him.

c. Read the following sentence:

A bright blue butterfly landed on the daisy.

A comma does not separate the adjectives *bright* and *blue,* because the words do not equally modify *butterfly*. To test words to see if they equally modify, try switching the words around or add *and* between the two adjectives.
Ex: A blue bright butterfly - does not sound right
A blue and bright butterfly - does not sound right

Also, when number words are used with another adjective, do **not** use a comma.
Ex: Five green frogs croaked in the pond.

Green five frogs - does not sound right
Five and green frogs - does not sound right

d. Add commas, as needed, to the following words:
1) A fresh colorful vase brightened the room.
2) Soft sweet music filled the air.
3) Five hungry children stared at me.
4) A shiny crisp apple sat by his plate.

e. Using the sentences above, underline the subject once and underline the verb twice. Draw an arrow from the adjective to the noun it describes.

f. Diagram only the subject, verb, and adjectives which are bolded. Remember to always diagram articles, possessive nouns, and possessive pronouns as adjectives.

1) **A fresh, colorful vase brightened** the room.
2) **Soft, sweet music filled** the air.
3) **Five hungry children stared** at me.
4) **A shiny, crisp apple sat** by his plate.

g. Optional: Take an oral or written spelling pretest.

5. a. Take the literature passage from dictation.

OR

   b. Practice locating adjectives in your easy-readers. Which ones are articles? Which ones are possessive pronouns? Which ones are possessive nouns?

OR

   c. Write your own sentences with adjectives.

OR

   d. Choose skills from the *Review Activities* on the next page.

1.
a. Her white <u>hair</u> <u><u>glistened</u></u>.
b. Three little <u>puppies</u> <u><u>whimpered</u></u>.
c. The old <u>lawnmower</u> <u><u>is</u></u> <u><u>working</u></u>.
d. Tom's <u>father</u> <u><u>laughed</u></u>.
e. My gold <u>watch</u> <u><u>broke</u></u>.

2.

a.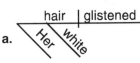

b.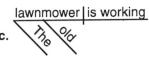

c.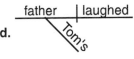

d.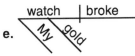

e.

3.
a. **Mark** had an appointment on **Friday** with **Dr. Samuel E. Barthe.**
b. **I** read the novel, *War and Peace* (War and Peace).
c. **Marcy** went to **Tennessee** to see the fall colors of **October.**
d. **Diamond** gave birth to six black and white puppies.
e. **Visiting Yellowstone National Park** was unforgettable.

Review Activities

Choose the skills your student needs to review.

1. *Subject and Verb*
   Underline the subject once and underline the verb twice.

   a. Her white hair glistened.
   b. Three little puppies whimpered.
   c. The old lawnmower is working.
   d. Tom's father laughed.
   e. My gold watch broke.

2. *Diagram - Subject, Verb, Adjectives*
   Using the sentences above, diagram each word in every sentence. Diagram the subject, verb, and adjective. Diagram pronouns, possessive nouns, and articles as adjectives.

3. *Capitalization and Punctuation*
   Add capitalization and punctuation to the following:

   a. mark had an appointment on friday with dr samuel e barthe.
   b. I read the novel, war and peace.
   c. marcy went to tennessee to see the fall colors of october.
   d. diamond gave birth to six black and white puppies.
   e. visiting yellowstone national park was unforgettable.

4. *Commas*
   Add commas.

   a. The long cold winter dragged on for months.
   b. Melissa added wholewheat pretzels glazed peanuts and fresh cashews to the party mix.
   c. We saw monkeys swinging on ropes polar bears playing in the water and alligators basking in the sun.
   d. The crippled old woman walked with a limp.
   e. Russell drove up in his shiny new convertible.

5. *Adjectives - Comparative & Superlative*
   Fill in the chart.

Positive	Comparative	Superlative
a. quiet		
b. joyful		
c. grand		
d. serious		
e. simple		

4.
a. **The long, cold winter dragged on for months.**
b. **Melissa added wholewheat pretzels, glazed peanuts, and fresh cashews to the party mix.**
c. **We saw monkeys swinging on ropes, polar bears playing in the water, and alligators basking in the sun.**
d. **The crippled, old woman walked with a limp.**
e. **Russell drove up in his shiny, new convertible.**

5.

	Comparative	Superlative
a.	quieter	quietest
b.	more joyful	most joyful
c.	more grand	most grand
d.	more serious	most serious
e.	simpler	simplest

Assessment 1
(Lessons 1 - 3)

1. Draw a vertical line between between the complete subject and the complete predicate. Underline the simple subject once and the verb twice.

    a. God spoke to Noah.
    b. Noah built the ark.
    c. The animals went into the ark.
    d. The rains came.
    e. God saved Noah and his family.

2. Write the definition of a noun.

3. Rewrite the following sentences, replacing appropriate pronouns for the underlined words:

God spoke to Moses out of the burning bush. <u>God</u> told Moses to go back to Egypt and tell Pharaoh, "Let My people go." Moses met <u>Moses'</u> brother Aaron on the way. <u>Moses and Aaron</u> went to Pharaoh. Pharaoh would not listen to <u>Moses and Aaron</u> because God hardened <u>Pharaoh's</u> heart.

4. Underline the pronoun and circle its antecedent in the following sentence:

Linda was so happy when she finally understood what had happened.

5. Write three sentences with an action verb.

6. Write three sentences with a state of being verb.

Left margin answer key:

1.
a. God / spoke to Noah.
b. Noah / built the ark.
c. The animals / went into the ark.
d. The rains / came.
e. God / saved Noah and his family.

2. A noun names a person, place, thing, or idea.

3. God spoke to Moses out of the burning bush. He told Moses to go back to Egypt and tell Pharaoh, "Let My people go." Moses met his brother Aaron on the way. They went to Pharaoh. Pharaoh would not listen to them because God hardened his heart.

✎Note: To retain clarity in a sentence, not all nouns should be replaced with pronouns.

4. (Linda) was so happy when she finally understood what had happened.

5. Answers will vary. Action verbs show what a person or thing does. Ex: The dog barked.

6. Answers will vary. Being verbs show what a person or thing is. am, is, are, was, were, be, being, been Ex: The dog is loud.

7. Diagram only the simple subject and verb in the sentences in **1a-e**. Not every word will be diagrammed.

8. Underline the adjectives and circle the articles in the following sentences. Tell what questions the adjectives answer:
   a. The small man climbed up the tree.
   b. The good teacher was coming.
   c. A great crowd surrounded Him.
   d. Two kind eyes looked up in the tree.
   e. A gentle, sweet voice called to him.

9. Write the comparative and superlative form of each of the adjectives you underlined above.

10. Diagram only the simple subject, verb, and adjectives in the sentences in **8a-e**. Not every word will be diagrammed.

7.
a. <u>God |spoke</u>
b. <u>Noah | built</u>
c. <u>animals |went</u>
d. <u>rains |came</u>
e. <u>God | saved</u>

8.
a. The (article), small (adjective, what kind), the (article)
b. The (article), good (adjective, what kind)
c. A (article), great (adjective, what kind)
d. Two (adjective, how many), kind (adjective, what kind), the (article)
e. A (article), gentle (adjective, what kind), sweet (adjective, what kind)

9.
Comparative	Superlative
a. smaller	smallest
b. better	best
c. greater	greatest
d. kinder	kindest
e. more gentle	most gentle
f. sweeter	sweetest

(Two) cannot be compared

10.

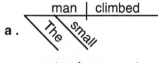

a. man | climbed / The \ small

b. teacher | was coming / The \ good

c. crowd | surrounded / A \ great

d. eyes | looked / Two \ kind

e. voice | called / A \ gentle \ sweet

27

The
Poetry Unit

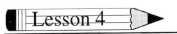
**The Poetry Unit is a
six-week unit.**

Poetry is an important part of your curriculum. Exploring poetry will increase your fluency and sensitivity to language in all your writing. You will develop self-confidence in writing and develop valuable problem solving skills as you explore figurative language and become aware of new relationships between people, things, and ideas.

Many of us are somewhat afraid of poetry, feeling we do not understand much of it. Take time during the next six weeks to read poetry aloud to each other, choosing poems that you understand and enjoy. You will "catch" each other's excitement as you share these favorites. Usually, at the end of each week, you will have the option of hearing recitations. Encourage each other to have something memorized to recite.

Throughout *The Poetry Unit*, write your poetry on a separate sheet of paper. Put these aside to use at the end of the unit. In Lesson 9, you will make a poetry booklet using the poetry you have written.

If you do not already have some books of poetry, go to the library and check out several to use during the following weeks. We recommend *Favorite Poems, Old and New* published by Bantam Doubleday Dell.

Poetry Appreciation

1. Begin looking through the books of poetry you have collected. Just as a song needs to be heard to be appreciated, poems also are written to appeal to the ear. Because of this you will find that you enjoy poetry more if you hear it. So read aloud to each other today. Do you find a certain poet you like best?

2. As you continue reading poetry aloud, you will discover poems you really like. It would be a good idea to begin memorizing them. This will help train your ear to the rhythm and beauty of poetry, and will also make these poems really yours for a lifetime.

   You may have difficulty choosing a poem to memorize. During this unit, there will be some suggested poems for you to memorize. You will usually be given two short poems or part of a longer poem. If you choose a long poem, you may wish to take two weeks to work on it instead of one. Remember, you can choose your own poem(s) or choose one or more of the suggested poems. The important thing is to work on memorizing throughout the week and be prepared to recite.

   Here are the suggested poems for this week:

   Count that Day Lost by George Eliot

   If you sit down at set of sun
   And count the acts that you have done,
   *   And, counting, find*
   One self-denying deed, one word
   That eased the heart of him who heard,
   *   One glance most kind*
   That fell like sunshine where it went—
   Then you may count that day well spent.

   But if, through all the livelong day,
   You've cheered no heart, by yea or nay—
   *   If, through it all*
   You've nothing done that you can trace

That brought the sunshine to one face—
    No act most small
That helped some soul and nothing cost—
Then count that day as worse than lost.

Can't by Edgar Guest

Can't is the worst word that's written or spoken;
    Doing more harm here than slander and lies;
On it is many a strong spirit broken,
    And with it many a good purpose dies.
It springs from the lips of the thoughtless each morning
    And robs us of courage we need through the day:
It rings in our ears like a timely sent warning
    And laughs when we falter and fall by the way.

Can't is the father of feeble endeavor,
    The parent of terror and halfhearted work;
It weakens the efforts of artisans clever,
    And makes of the toiler an indolent shirk.
It poisons the soul of the man with a vision,
    It stifles in infancy many a plan;
It greets honest toiling with open derision
    And mocks at the hopes and the dreams of a man.

Can't is a word none should speak without blushing;
    To utter it should be a symbol of shame;
Ambition and courage it daily is crushing;
    It blights a man's purpose and shortens his aim.
Despise it with all of your hatred of error;
    Refuse it the lodgment it seeks in your brain;
Arm against it as a creature of terror,
    And all that you dream of you someday shall gain.

Can't is the word that is foe to ambition,
    An enemy ambushed to shatter your will;
Its prey is forever the man with a mission
    And bows but to courage and patience and skill.
Hate it, with hatred that's deep and undying,
    For once it is welcomed 'twill break any man;
Whatever the goal you are seeking, keep trying
    And answer this demon by saying: "I can."

The following is only part of a longer poem. You may wish to learn all or part of it.

The Highwayman by Alfred Noyes

The wind was a torrent of darkness among the gusty trees,
The moon was a ghostly galleon tossed upon cloudy seas,
The road was a ribbon of moonlight over the purple moor—
And the highwayman came riding—riding—riding
The highwayman came riding, up to the old inn-door.

He'd a French cocked-hat on his forehead, a bunch of lace at his chin,
A coat of the claret velvet, and breeches of brown doe-skin;
They fitted with never a wrinkle; his boots were up to the thigh!
And he rode with a jeweled twinkle,
His pistol butts a-twinkle,
His rapier hilt a-twinkle, under the jeweled sky.

3.   Continue reading poetry aloud. Spend some time memorizing. If you have found a poet to be a favorite, learn something about his or her life.

4.   Continue reading poetry aloud and memorizing. Practice reciting your poem using good expression.

5.   Recitation Day. Follow these guidelines when giving a recitation.

Tips on Recitation

1. Begin by stating the title and author of your poem.
2. No gum chewing allowed.
3. Stand straight and tall with hands to your side.
4. Look straight ahead; not at the floor.
5. Speak clearly and slowly.
6. Use good expression.

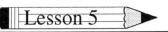

Imagery

1. a. **Imagery** is the use of vivid description to appeal to the reader's sense of sight, hearing, smell, taste, or touch. The pictures or sensations produced in the reader's mind are images of the real thing. The reader's imagination enables him to form these images in his mind.

   Writers use **figurative language** in order to accomplish this imaging. We are going to focus on three types of figurative language:
   - simile
   - metaphor
   - personification

   b. Read the following poem by Sir Walter Scott aloud.

   The tear down childhood's cheek that flows
   *Is **like** the dew-drop on the rose;*
   When next the summer breeze comes by
   And waves the bush, the flower is dry.

   c. A **simile** gives an idea or image of something by comparing it to something else using the connecting word *like* or *as*.

   Can you find the simile in Sir Walter Scott's poem?

   d. Read the following poem aloud. This is the first verse of a longer poem.

   Hearth by Peggy Bacon

   A cat sat quaintly by the fire
   And watched the burning coals
   And watched the little flames aspire
   Like small decrepit souls.

   e. Find the simile.

   f. Write a sentence comparing two things using a simile. Explain how they are similar.

Sidebar answers:

1.
c. The tear is *like* the dew-drop

e. Flames aspire *like* small decrepit souls.

f. Answers will vary.

g. Here are the suggested poems for this week's memorization:

Trees by Joyce Kilmer

I think that I shall never see
A poem lovely as a tree.

A tree whose hungry mouth is pressed
Against the earth's sweet flowing breast;

A tree that looks at God all day
And lifts her leafy arms to pray;

A tree that may in summer wear
A nest of robins in her hair;

Upon whose bosom snow has lain;
Who intimately lives with rain.

Poems are made by fools like me,
But only God can make a tree.

A Narrow Fellow in the Grass by Emily Dickinson

A narrow fellow in the grass
Occasionally rides;
You may have met him,—did you not?
His notice sudden is.

The grass divides as with a comb,
A spotted shaft is seen;
And then it closes at your feet
And opens further on.

He loves a boggy acre,
A floor too cool for corn.
Yet when a child, and barefoot,
I more than once, at morn,

Have passed, I thought a whip-lash
Unbraiding in the sun,—
When stooping to secure it,
it wrinkled, and was gone.

Several of nature's people
I know, and they know me;
I feel for them a transport
Of cordiality—;

But never met this fellow,
Attended or alone,
Without a tighter breathing,
And zero at the bone.

Here's part of a longer poem for you to try:

The Spider and the Fly by Mary Howitt

"Will you walk into my parlor?" said the Spider to the Fly,
"'Tis the prettiest little parlor that ever you did spy;
The way into my parlor is up a winding stair,
And I have many curious things to show when you are there."
"Oh no, no," said the little Fly, "to ask me is in vain;
For who goes up your winding stair can ne'er come down again."

"I'm sure you must be weary, dear, with soaring up so high;
Will you rest upon my little bed?" said the Spider to the Fly.
"There are pretty curtains drawn around, the sheets are fine and thin;
And if you like to rest awhile, I'll snugly tuck you in!"
"Oh no, no," said the little Fly, "for I've often heard it said
They never, never wake again, who sleep upon your bed!"

2.
a. Possible answers:
1) I'm as straight as a pin.
2) I fit like a glove.
3) I'm as soft as the clouds.
4) I'm as sticky as sap.

2. a. Today you will do some activities that will help you practice comparing things. Write simile sentence clues that describe by telling about the size, color, shape, smell, taste, weight, sound, or touch of an object. Try to write more than one clue for each of the following objects. Remember, you want to appeal to the reader's senses.
Ex: apple
I'm as big as a croquet ball. (size)
I'm as red as a rose. (color)

1) pencil
2) shoe
3) marshmallow
4) glue

b. Use similes to make your verbs more expressive.
   Ex: The sailboats <u>bobbed</u> (action verb) on the lake *like* <u>bottle corks</u> (noun).

   1) The rain _____ on the roof *like* _____.
   2) The wind _____ in the trees *like* _____.
   3) The cat _____ on the fence *like* _____.
   4) The light _____ on the water *like* _____.

c. Many similes that first come to mind are common sayings we hear quite often. For example, have you ever heard or said the following?

   > He's as brave as a lion.
   > She's as quiet as a mouse.

   These are called **cliches**. A cliche is an overused expression or image. When writing poetry, try to avoid cliches.

d. Using the following list of adjectives, write a common expression for each one, then try to write a fresh, new simile for each.
   1) soft as
   2) cute as
   3) cold as
   4) brave as
   5) white as

e. If you have time, spend the rest of the time observing the figurative language in your poetry books.

3. a. Yesterday you did some activities with similes. Today you will practice writing metaphor and personification.

   Read the following poetry excerpt aloud:

   My Bed is a Boat by Robert Louis Stevenson

   My bed is a little boat;
   Nurse helps me in when I embark
   She girds me in my sailor's coat
   And starts me in the dark.

2.
b.Possible answers:
1) The rain <u>pitter -pattered</u> on the roof *like* <u>tiny feet</u>.
2) The wind <u>whispered</u> in the trees *like* <u>a lullabye</u>.
3) The cat <u>stalked</u> on the fence *like* <u>a prowler</u>.
4) The light <u>glistened</u> on the water *like* <u>diamonds</u>.

2.
d.Possible answers:
1) a feather (cliche)
   a billowy cloud
2) a button (cliche)
   a newborn babe
3) ice (cliche)
   a frosty morning
4) a lion (cliche)
   a knight
5) snow (cliche)
   wool

A **metaphor** is a comparison in which one thing is said to be another. A comparison is made by using any form of the verb *be* (being, been, been, is, am, are, was, were).

3.
b. My bed is a little boat. The poetry line compares the bed with a boat.

b. Find the metaphor in the previous poem.

c. Read the following poetry excerpt.

The Covenant by William Cowper

The Lord proclaims his grace abroad;
Behold, I change your hearts of stone;
Each shall renounce his idol god,
And serve, henceforth, the Lord alone.

My grace, a flowing stream, proceeds
To wash your filthiness away;
Ye shall abhor your former deeds,
And learn my statutes to obey.

An **implied metaphor** is a comparison that does not use any form of the verb *be*.

Can you find the implied metaphor in "The Covenant?"

c. Hearts of stone
My grace, a flowing stream

d. Read the following poetry excerpt.

Prayer for a Blessing by William Cowper

Grace is a plant, where'er it grows,
Of pure and heav'nly root;
But fairest in the youngest shews,
And yields the sweetest fruit.

e. "Grace is a plant" expresses a metaphor. Grace is said to be a plant.

e. Does the poem above express a metaphor or an implied metaphor? Why?

f. We sometimes confuse simile and metaphor. The following example illustrates how we can write a basic comparison and express it as a simile, a metaphor, or an implied metaphor.

Ex: Your word is *like* a lamp unto my feet. (simile)
    Your word *is* a lamp unto my feet. (metaphor)
    The *lamp of your word* lights my path. (implied metaphor)

g. Write the following simile as a metaphor and an implied metaphor and label each appropriately:

    Her heart is like a garden.

h. Using your work from **2a - e**, rewrite some of your similes as complete sentences, and then write them again as a metaphor or implied metaphor.

4. a. Read the following poem.

    Out of the bosom of the air,
    Out of the cloud-folds of her garment shaken,
    Over the woodlands brown and bare,
    Over the harvest-fields forsaken,
    Silent, and soft, and slow
    Descends the snow.

    Personification is comparing an object to a living thing. The writer is not saying "This is like this" but instead "This behaves like a person."
    Ex: The wind *muttered* through the quiet oaks.

    b. Find the personification used in the poem above.

    c. Read the following poem.

    Autumn by Emily Dickinson

    The morns are meeker than they were,
    *   The nuts getting brown;*
    The berry's cheek is plumper,
    *   The rose is out of town.*

    The maple wears a gayer scarf,
    *   The field a scarlet gown.*
    Lest I should be old-fashioned,
    *   I'll put a trinket on.*

3.
g. Her heart is a garden. - metaphor
Possible answer:
Her heart, a garden, quaint and sweet. - implied metaphor

h. Possible answers:
The baby's blanket is as soft as a billowy cloud. (simile)
The baby's blanket is a soft billowy cloud. (metaphor)
The baby's blanket, a soft billowy cloud, caresses her as she sleeps. (implied metaphor)

4.
b. Out of the bosom of the air, Out of the cloud-folds of her garment shaken,

4.

**d. morns are meeker,
berry's cheek, rose is
out of town, maple wears
a gayer scarf, field a
scarlet gown.**

e. Possible answers:
2) danced
3) protected
4) whispered

f. Answers will vary

5.
a. Answers will vary.

5.
c. Answers will vary.

d. Find examples of personification in "Autumn."

e. Look at the following statements:

1) The stairs *made noise.*
2) A sparrow *flew by.*
3) The tree *covered* the boy.
4) The light *came* through the trees.

Pretend that each of these things move or talk or act like a person. Change the italicized words to show the object acting like a person.
Ex: The stairs *groaned.*

f. Find examples of a metaphor and personification in your poetry reading today.

5. Most of the poetry you have been reading probably rhymed. The poems you write today will not. Concentrate on word images by using simile, metaphor, or personification as studied during the last few days.

Choose one or more of the following "poem starters":

a. Choosing one subject, write a poem that uses similes that appeal to at least three senses.
Ex:
*While walking on the shore one day
The air smelled sharp <u>like tar,</u> (smell)
And the sand shone <u>like a heap of gold</u> (sight)
As it sparkled from afar.
The waves broke in upon the beach
<u>Like an angry lion's roar,</u> (hearing)
Then tiptoed quietly back out
Only to return once more.*

b. Write a poem from an object's point of view. Show what the object may think and how it may feel.
Ex:
*I am short and very stout,
with legs bowed at the knee.
I'm often pushed and moved about,
and people stand on me.*

I make a handy foot rest.
I do not jump or bark,
But when it's night beware lest
you trip on me in the dark.

This poem was written from *a stool's* point of view.

c. Choose a color and write a poem describing it using a simile
    and/or a metaphor.

    Ex:
    Purple is a mighty King, (metaphor)
    with scepter and glowing crown.
    While Pink is like a pretty queen, (simile)
    with soft and flowing gown.

d. Choose an activity you are familiar with (playing football,
    sailing, playing a musical instrument, horseback riding, etc.)
    and write a poem describing how you feel when you are
    doing the activity.

    Ex:
    Basketball

    The whistle blows
    The referee throws
    The ball up in the air.
    The players jump.
    We hear a thump,
    And the ball flies over there.
    The players fall.
    They pass the ball.
    They all are in a sweat.
    Some people cheer,
    While others sneer,
    As the ball goes through the net.
    The game is done.
    One side has won.
    The teams shake hands together.
    What fun is had.
    We all are glad
    For a ball made out of leather.

d. Answers will vary.

Structural Poems

1. a. This week you will be learning and using some common poetry forms:
   1) haiku   2) cinquain
   3) diamante   4) limerick

   These poems conform to a particular pattern that can be copied.

   Haiku, the simple Japanese form of poetry, consists of three unrhymed lines, usually containing 17 syllables. The first line contains 5 syllables, the second line contains 7 syllables, and the third line contains 5 syllables. The poem usually deals with nature, very often giving some idea of the season and may contain a surprise at the end.
   Ex:
   Snail, my little man, (5 syllables)
   Slowly - ah, very slowly, (7 syllables)
   Climb up Mount Fuji! (5 syllables)

   If possible find some examples of haiku to read before writing your own. Spend the rest of your time today writing haiku. Think of topics from nature, such as the weather, the seasons, plants, or animals. Don't forget your memorization work.

   b. This week's suggestions contain some humorous works:

   Eletelephony by Laura E. Richards

   Once there was an elephant,
   Who tried to use the telephant—
   No! no! I mean an elephone
   Who tried to use the telephone—
   (Dear me! I am not certain quite
   That even now I've got it right.)

   Howe'er it was, he got his trunk
   Entangled in the telephunk;
   The more he tried to get it free,
   The louder buzzed the telephee—
   (I fear I'd better drop the song
   Of elephop and telephong!)

Enjoy the nonsense words in this famous poem by Lewis Carroll.

Jabberwocky by Lewis Carroll

'Twas brillig, and the slithy toves
Did gyre and gimble in the wabe:
All mimsy were the borogoves,
And the mome raths outgrabe.

"Beware the Jabberwock, my son!
The jaws that bite, the claws that catch!
Beware the Jubjub bird, and shun
The frumious Bandersnatch!"

He took his vorpal sword in hand:
Long time the manxome foe he sought—
So rested he by the Tumtum tree
And stood awhile in thought.

And, as in uffish thought he stood,
The Jabberwock, with eyes of flame,
Came whiffling through the tulgey wood,
And burbled as it came!

One, two! One, two! And through and through
The vorpal blade went snicker-snack!
He left it dead, and with its head
He went galumphing back.

"And hast thou slain the Jabberwock?
Come to my arms, my beamish boy!
O frabjous day! Callooh! Callay!"
He chortled in his joy.

'Twas brillig, and the slithy toves
Did gyre and gimble in the wabe:
All mimsy were the borogoves,
And the mome raths outgrabe.

Finally, here is part of a longer poem:

Casey at the Bat by Ernest Lawrence Thayer

The outlook wasn't brilliant for the Mudville nine that day;
The score stood four to two with but one inning more to play.
And then when Cooney died at first and Barrows did the same,
A sickly silence fell upon the patrons of the game.

A straggling few got up to go in deep despair. The rest
Clung to the hope which springs eternal in the human breast;
They thought if only Casey could but get a whack at that—
We'd put up even money now with Casey at the bat.

2.   The **cinquain** is another poetry form using a different pattern:
Ex:
Caterpillar (one-word topic)
Plump, Fat, (two adjectives describing the topic)
Creeping, Crawling, Eating (three verbs telling what the topic does)
Spins a little cocoon (a thought about the one-word topic)
Butterfly (same one-word topic OR synonym or related word)

(Melissa Burger, age 12)

Write your own cinquain following the directions below.

Line 1 - Write a noun or any topic in one word.
Line 2 - Write two adjectives describing the noun, and
           separate them by a comma.
Line 3 - Write three verbs that tell what the noun or topic, on
           Line 1 does. Separate them by commas.
Line 4 - Write a thought about the word you wrote on the
           Line 1. This should be a short phrase (4-5 words)
           expressing a feeling.
Line 5 - Write the word from Line 1, a synonym or a related
           word.

3.   The **diamante** poem derives its name from the diamond
     shape it creates using the following the directions:

     Line 1 - Write a noun. Line 7 will be an antonym for this word.
     Line 2 - Write two adjectives describing the noun on line 1.
     Line 3 - Write three verbs ending in **-ing** describing the word
              from line 1.
     Line 4 - Write two nouns relating to or describing the word
              from line 1 and two nouns that relate to or describe
              the antonym on line 7.
     Line 5 - Write three participles ending in **-ing** that describe
              the word from line 7.
     Line 6 - Write two adjectives describing the word from line 7.
     Line 7 - Write an antonym for the word from line 1.

     Write your own diamante in the shape of a diamond.
     Look at the diagram below:

                         Bird
                    Beautiful, Red
                Flying, Singing, Eating
               Clouds, Sky, Paws, Fur
              Running, Jumping, Pouncing
                    Sly, Cautious
                         Cat
                 (Katherine Welch, Age 12)

4.   The final, and perhaps most familiar poetry form you will use
     this week is the **limerick**, a humorous verse of five lines.
     Read aloud some limericks and listen to the cadence or
     rhythm of the lines.

Limericks usually follow this pattern:

Lines l, 2, and 5 rhyme.
Lines 3 and 4 rhyme.
Lines l, 2, and 5 usually have from 8 to 10 syllables.
Lines 3 and 4 usually have from 5 to 7 syllables.
Typically the first line introduces the character.

Ex:
There was a young lady of Niger
Who smiled as she rode on a tiger,
They returned from the ride
With the lady inside,
And the smile on the face of the tiger.

Write your own limericks following the above pattern.

5. a. If you have especially enjoyed any of the structured poems
        this week, continue writing, or spend some time again
        reading poetry aloud.

    b. Recite the poem(s) you memorized this week. Perhaps you
        would like to recite the ones you wrote, too!

Writing Poetry Using a Model

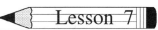

1. a. Poems that rhyme often follow a consistent **rhyme scheme** or pattern. To identify the scheme, we label the ending sounds of each line. Those that rhyme have the same label. Read the following poem aloud.

The Wind by Robert Louis Stevenson

I saw you toss the kites on <u>high</u>	**(a)**
And blow the birds about the <u>sky</u>;	**(a)**
And all around I heard you <u>pass</u>,	**(b)**
Like ladies' skirts across the <u>grass</u>—	**(b)**
O wind, a-blowing all day <u>long</u>,	**(c)**
O wind, that sings so loud a <u>song</u>!	**(c)**
I saw the different things you <u>did</u>,	**(a)**
But always you yourself you <u>hid</u>.	**(a)**
I felt you push, I heard you <u>call</u>,	**(b)**
I could not see yourself at <u>all</u>—	**(b)**
O wind, a-blowing all day <u>long</u>,	**(c)**
O wind, that sings so loud a <u>song</u>!	**(c)**
O you that are so strong and <u>cold</u>,	**(a)**
O blower, are you young or <u>old</u>?	**(a)**
Are you a beast of field or <u>tree</u>,	**(b)**
Or just a stronger child than <u>me</u>?	**(b)**
O wind, a-blowing all day <u>long</u>,	**(c)**
O wind, that sings so loud a <u>song</u>!	**(c)**

This poem has a rhyme scheme **aabbcc**.

b. Read the following poem:

Winter by Alfred Lord Tennyson

The frost is here,	**(a)**
And fuel is dear,	**(a)**
And woods are sear,	**(a)**
And fires burn clear,	**(a)**
And frost is here	**(a)**
And has bitten the heel of the going year.	**(a)**

Bite, frost, bite!	**(b)**
You roll up away from the light	**(b)**
The blue wood-louse, and the plump dormouse,	**(c)**
And the bees are still'd, and the flies are kill'd,	**(d)**
And you bite far into the heart of the house,	**(c)**
But not into mine.	**(e)**

Bite, frost, bite!	**(b)**
The woods are all the searer,	**(f)**
The fuel is all the dearer,	**(f)**
The fires are all the clearer,	**(f)**
My spring is all the nearer,	**(f)**
You have bitten into the heart of the earth,	**(g)**
But not into mine.	**(e)**

c. Two of this week's suggested poems have a nautical theme:

Sea Fever by John Masefield

I must go down to the sea again, to the lonely sea and the sky,
And all I ask is a tall ship and a star to steer her by,
And the wheel's kick and the wind's song and the white sail's shaking,
And a gray mist on the sea's face, and a gray dawn breaking.

I must go down to the seas again, for the call of the running tide
Is a wild call and a clear call that may not be denied;
An all I ask is a windy day with the white clouds flying,
And the flung spray and the blown spume, and the sea gulls crying.

I must go down to the seas again, to the vagrant gypsy life,
To the gull's way and the whale's way where the wind's like a
    whetted knife;
And all I ask is a merry yarn from a laughing fellow-rover,
And quiet sleep and a sweet dream when the long trick's over.

d. Read the following poem about Columbus' famous voyage:

Sail on! Sail on! by Joaquin Miller

Behind him lay the gray Azores,
    Behind the gates of Hercules;
Before him not the ghost of shores,
    Before him only shoreless seas.
The good mate said: "Now must we pray,
    For lo! the very stars are gone;
Speak, Admiral, what shall I say?"
    "Why say, sail on! and on!"

"My men grow mut'nous day by day;
    My men grow ghastly wan and weak."
The stout mate thought of home; a spray
    Of salt wave wash'd his swarthy cheek.
"What shall I say, brave Admiral,
    If we sight naught but seas at dawn?"
"Why, you shall say, at break of day:
    'Sail on! sail on! and on!'"

They sailed and sailed, as winds might blow
    Until at last the blanch'd mate said:
"Why, now, not even God would know
    Should I and all my men fall dead.
These very winds forget their way,
    For God from these dread seas is gone.
No speak, brave Admiral, and say—"
    He said: "Sail on! and on!"

They said, they sailed, then spoke his mate:
    "This mad sea shows his teeth tonight,
He curls his lip, he lies in wait,
    With lifted teeth as if to bite!
Brave Admiral, say but one word;
    What shall we do when hope is gone?"
The words leaped as a leaping sword:
    "Sail on! sail on! and on!"

Then, pale and worn, he kept his deck,
    and thro' the darkness peered that night.

Ah, darkest night! and then a speck—
  A light! a light! a light! a light!
It grew—a star-lit flag unfurled!
  It grew to be Time's burst of dawn;
He gained a world! he gave that world
  Its watchword: "On! and on!"

e. The following longer narrative is a poem about another exciting time in our nation's history. Again, only part of the poem is given.

The Little Black-Eyed Rebel by Will Carleton

A boy drove into the city, his wagon loaded down
With food to feed the people of the British-governed town;
And the little black-eyed rebel, so innocent and sly,
Was watching for his coming from the corner of her eye.

His face looked broad and honest, his hands were brown and tough,
The clothes he wore upon him were homespun, coarse, and rough;
But one there was who watched him, who long time lingered nigh
And cast at him sweet glances from the corner of her eye.

2. a. When listening to poetry we usually hear the syllables of a line in groups of two's or three's. For example, if we stress the first syllable of a word but not the next, the rhythm sounds like DUMM-de DUMM-de, etc. We can mark it like this to show a stressed syllable: (´); and an unstressed syllable: (⌣). Each of these rhythmic units is called a **foot**.

There are four basic feet in English verse:
iambic - de-DUMM (⌣ ´)
anapestic - de-de-DUMM (⌣ ⌣ ´)
trochaic - DUMM-de (´ ⌣)
dactylic - DUMM -de-de (´ ⌣ ⌣)

For example, using Stevenson's poem, "The Wind" that we analyzed yesterday, the poem's rhythm is in the iambic foot (unstressed syllable, stressed syllable). It is important to remember that poets very often depart from strict metrical patterns. When you scan verses you are just looking for a basic pattern. Also, two readers may scan the same lines in quite different ways.

b. Scan the following poem.

The Kitten at Play by William Wordsworth

See the kitten on the wall,
Sporting with the leaves that fall,
Withered leaves, one, two and three
Falling from the elder tree,
Through the calm and frosty air
Of the morning bright and fair.

See the kitten, how she starts,
Crouches, stretches, paws and darts;
With a tiger-leap half way
Now she meets her coming prey.
Lets it go as fast and then
Has it in her power again.

Now she works with three and four,
Like an Indian conjurer;
Quick as he in feats of art,
Gracefully she plays her part;
Yet were gazing thousands there;
What would little Tabby care?

c. What is the poem's rhyme scheme and rhythmic foot?

3. a. Read the following poem.

Autumn Fancies (Anonymous)

The maple is a dainty maid,
*   The pet of all the wood,*
Who lights the dusky forest glade
*   With scarlet cloak and hood.*

The elm a lovely lady is,
*   In shimmering robes of gold,*
That catch the sunlight when she moves,
*   And glisten, fold on fold.*

The sumac is a gypsy queen,
*   Who flaunts in crimson dressed,*
And wild along the roadside runs,
*   Red blossoms in her breast.*

2.
c. rhyme scheme - aabbcc
**   rhythmic foot - trochaic**

51

And towering high above the wood,
    All in his purple cloak,
A monarch in his splendor is
    The proud and princely oak.

3.
c. rhyme scheme
   1st stanza - abab
   2nd - 4th stanza - abcb
   rhythmic foot - iambic

b. Today, use "Autumn Fancies" as a model to write your own poem about different kinds of flowers, birds, etc. Or, you may choose to add another stanza to the poem above.

c. Before you begin writing, analyze the poem. What is its rhyme scheme? What is its rhythmic foot? Your lines should follow the same pattern.

4. a. Read the following poem. Only part of the poem is given.

My Evening Prayer by Charles H. Gabriel

If I have wounded any soul today,
If I have caused one foot to go astray,
If I have walked in my own wilful way—
Good Lord, forgive!

If I have uttered idle words or vain,
If I have turned aside from want or pain,
Lest I myself should suffer through the strain—
Good Lord, forgive!

4.
b. Rhyme scheme:
   lst stanza   aaab
   2nd stanza   cccb
   Rhythmic foot - iambic

b. Analyze the rhyme scheme and rhythmic foot of the first two stanzas.

Use the two stanzas above as a model, and try writing another stanza of this poem.

5. a. Choose another poem to use as a model, or write another verse to an existing poem.

b. Recite the poem(s) you have memorized this week.

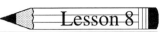
Psalms

1. a. We find some of the most beautiful poetry in the Bible, in the book of Psalms. The Psalms were poems that were sung. Some of the things they expressed were praise to God, confession of fear or sin, and thanksgiving.

   Psalm 29 (NASB)

   Ascribe to the Lord, O sons of the mighty,
   Ascribe to the Lord glory and strength.
   Ascribe to the Lord the glory due to His name;
   Worship the Lord in holy array.

   The voice of the Lord is upon the waters;
   The god of glory thunders,
   The Lord is over many waters.
   The voice of the Lord is powerful,
   The voice of the Lord is majestic.
   The voice of the Lord breaks the cedars;
   Yes, the Lord breaks in pieces the cedars of Lebanon.
   And He makes Lebanon skip like a calf,
   And Sirion like a young wild ox.
   The voice of the Lord hews out flames of fire.
   The voice of the Lord shakes the wilderness;
   The Lord shakes the wilderness of Kadesh.
   The voice of the Lord makes the deer to calve,
   And strips the forests bare,
   And in His temple everything says, "Glory!"

   *The Lord sat as **King** at the flood;*
   Yes, the Lord sits as King forever.
   The Lord will give strength to His people;
   The Lord will bless His people with peace.

   b. Notice the form of the Psalm. It is written in poetry form. Can you find any similes?

   c. Sometimes the Psalmist uses a repetitive word or phrase in a Psalm. What words are repeated in Psalm 29?

1.

b. Lebanon skip like a calf
Sirion like a young wild ox

c. Ascribe to the Lord, The voice of the Lord

1.
d. The repetition creates rhythm and shows emphasis.

f. Answers will vary.

d. What effect does this have?

e. Here is another well-known Psalm that uses a repeating phrase.

Psalm 136:1-4 (NASB)

Give thanks to the Lord, for He is good;
For His lovingkindness is everlasting.
Give thanks to the God of gods,
For His lovingkindness is everlasting.
Give thanks to the Lord of lords,
For His lovingkindness is everlasting.
To Him Who alone does great wonders,
For His lovingkindness is everlasting.

f. This pattern continues throughout the Psalm. Do you think it has a pleasing rhythm? Read a few Psalms today. Note any repeating phrases or words.

g. Here are two poems you may enjoy memorizing:

The Creation by Cecil Alexander

All things bright and beautiful,
*   All creatures great and small,*
All things wise and wonderful,
*   The Lord God made them all.*

Each little flower that opens,
*   Each little bird that sings,*
He made their glowing colors,
*   He made their tiny wings.*

The purple-headed mountain,
*   The river running by,*
The sunset, and the morning,
*   That brighten up the sky;*

The cold wind in the winter,
*   The pleasant summer sun,*
The ripe fruits in the garden,
*   He made them every one.*

The tall trees in the greenwood,
    The meadows where we play,
The rushes by the water,
    We gather every day;

He gave us eyes to see them,
    And lips that we might tell
How great is God Almighty,
    Who has made all things well.

A Psalm of Life by Henry Wadsworth Longfellow

Tell me not, in mournful numbers,
    Life is but an empty dream!—
For the soul is dead that slumbers,
    And things are not what they seem.

Life is real! Life is earnest!
    And the grave is not its goal;
Dust thou art, to dust returnest,
    Was not spoken of the soul.

Not enjoyment, and not sorrow,
    Is our destined end or way;
But to act, that each tomorrow
    Find us farther than today.

Art is long, and Time is fleeting,
    And our hearts, though stout and brave,
Still, like muffled drums, are beating
    Funeral marches to the grave.

In the world's broad field of battle,
    In the bivouac of Life,
Be not like dumb, driven cattle!
    Be a hero in the strife!

Trust no Future, howe'er pleasant!
    Let the dead Past bury its dead!
Act—act in the living Present!
    Heart within, and God o'erhead!

Lives of great men all remind us
        We can make our lives sublime,
And, departing, leave behind us
        Footprints on the sands of time;

Footprints, that perhaps another,
        Sailing o'er life's solemn main,
A forlorn and shipwrecked brother,
        Seeing, shall take heart again.

Let us, then, be up and doing,
        With a heart for any fate;
Still achieving, still pursuing,
        Learn to labor and to wait.

2. a. We find many examples of figurative language in the Psalms. The following Psalm speaks of a childlike trust in the Lord.

Psalm 131 (NASB)

O Lord, my heart is not proud, nor my eyes haughty;
Nor do I involve myself in great matters,
Or in things too difficult for me.
Surely I have composed and quieted my soul;
Like a weaned child rests against his mother,
My soul is like a weaned child within me.
O Israel, hope in the Lord
From this time forth and forever.

    b. What does the Psalmist compare to his soul?

2.
b. The psalmist compares his soul to a weaned child.

c. The following Psalm speaks of brotherly unity. Notice the rich imagery used.

Psalm 133 (NASB)

Behold, how good and how pleasant it is
For brothers to dwell together in unity!
It is like the precious oil upon the head,
Coming down upon the beard,
Even Aaron's beard,
Coming down upon the edge of his robes.
It is like the dew of Hermon,
Coming down upon the mountains of Zion;
For there the Lord commanded the blessing
—life forever.

Read some Psalms today noting simile and metaphor used.

3. Scripture exhorts us to *"...be filled with the Spirit; speaking to yourselves in psalms..."* (Eph. 5:18-19). Today you will begin writing a psalm of your own.

You may choose to use a repeating phrase as we read in **1a and 1e**. You could express your joy in remembering what God has done in the past and your confidence in what He will do in the future. Your psalm could be an expression of gratitude for benefits God has given you such as forgiveness, peace, confidence, protection, provision, and deliverance. Your psalm could express a need or a cry for help in troubled times.

It may also be helpful to use some of the key phrases that David used to express his need for God, such as *"I lift up my soul to Thee,"* *"I cry unto Thee,"* *"Thy face, Lord, will I seek."* Find other key phrases as you read through the Psalms.

Here is a psalm written by Erin Welch, age 10:

I shall be satisfied when I awake with Thy likeness.
I shall be satisfied when I walk in Thy presence.
I shall be satisfied when Thy face looketh well upon me.

The arm of the Lord is bold and just.
The arm of the Lord made the heavens and the earth.
The earth trembled when the Lord set His foot upon it.
The earth quaked and its mountains smoked when the Lord spoke.

Good and upright is the Lord and worthy of praise.
Let the nations laud Him.
Let the name of the Lord be praised.
I shall praise the Lord on the mountains.
I shall praise the Lord in the valleys.
I shall lift the name of the Lord on high!

Great is the Lord and worthy of honor.
Great is the name of the Lord.
Great is the Lord who is worthy of praise.

I shall enter His courts with thanksgiving in my heart.
I shall enter His courts with praise.
I shall honor the name of my King.
Praise the Lord!

4. You may continue working on your psalm or if you finished it, try choosing another theme. Read your psalm(s) out loud. You will also enjoy memorizing them.

5. a. Finish writing your psalms.

   b. Recite your psalm(s) and poem(s) to each other.

Finishing Up

1. All writers, even poets, go through a process of **revising** and **editing** their writing. This is hard work, but well worth it. Why should you spend time revising and editing your work? First of all, when you care about what you have written, you want it to be your very best effort. Sometimes, when we are quickly getting our thoughts down on paper or searching for a rhyme, we write down our first thoughts. Later, as we have time to think about what we have written, we find it is not exactly what we meant.

   For example, a student was given the assignment to write a poem modeled after Irene Rutherford McLeod's poem "Lone Dog." She chose to write about a deer.

   I'm a sleek deer, a meek deer, a fast deer and brown.
   I'm a shy deer, a spry deer, pounding o'er the ground.

   You will notice that these lines rhyme, but there is another rhyme within each line, *sleek/meek* and *shy/spry*. This is called an **internal rhyme**.

   When she came to the third line, she needed another internal rhyme.

   I'm a hasty deer, a tasty deer, running all the day.
   I love to jump and leap on logs, and watch the little fawns play.

   When we discussed the poem we both decided that while "a hasty deer, a tasty deer" was a good rhyme, it didn't exactly convey the idea she had in mind. It made you think of eating the deer. She got out a thesaurus and revised her poem.

   I'm a running deer, a cunning deer, running all the day.

   You cannot hope to improve your writing if you think it cannot be changed once it is written down. It can be very difficult to read your own work with an objective eye. Since writing is such hard work, we tend to become very attached to what we have written. You may find it helpful to talk over your work with your teacher. Some questions you can discuss are:

1) Have I really said what I meant to say?
2) Have I chosen words that express my intent clearly?
3) How can my work be improved?

Choose one of the poems you have written. Read it aloud. Does it need some revision to make it better? Read it aloud to your teacher. Discuss the poem. Make any changes you feel will improve the poem. For example, you may want to change, add, or drop a word or line.

I hope you enjoy the following suggested poems for memorization:

The Quality of Mercy by William Shakespeare

The quality of mercy is not strain'd.
It droppeth as the gentle rain from heaven
Upon the place beneath. It is twice blest:
It blesseth him that gives, and him that takes.
'Tis mightiest in the mightiest; it becomes
The throned monarch better than his crown.
His scepter shows the force of temporal power,
The attribute to awe and majesty,
Wherein doth sit the dread and fear of kings;
But mercy is above this sceptered sway;
It is enthroned in the hearts of kings;
It is an attribute to God himself;
And earthly power doth then show likest God's
When mercy seasons justice.

The Touch of the Master's Hand by Myra Brooks Welch

'Twas battered and scarred, and the auctioneer
Thought it scarcely worth his while
To waste much time on the old violin,
But he held it up with a smile;
"What am I bidden, good folk?" he cried,
"Who'll start the bidding for me?
A dollar - one dollar- two, only two -
Two dollars, and who'll make it three?
Going for three" - but no -
From the room far back, a grayhaired man
Came forward and picked up the bow;

Then wiping the dust from the old violin,
And tightening the loosened strings,
He played a melody pure and sweet
As a caroling angel sings.
The music ceased and the auctioneer,
With a voice that was quiet and low,
Said, "Now what am I bid for the old violin?"
And he held it up with the bow;
"A thousand dollars - and who'll make it two?
Two thousand and who'll make it three?
Three thousand once - three thousand twice -
and going - and gone," cried he;
The people cheered, but some of them cried,
"We do not quite understand;
What changed its worth?" Quick came the reply,
"The touch of the master's hand."

And many a man with life out of tune,
and battered and scarred with sin,
Is auctioned cheap to a thoughtless crowd,
Much like the old violin;
A mess of pottage - a glass of wine,
A game - and he travels on;
He's going once - and going twice -
He's going - and almost gone!
But the Master comes, and the foolish crowd
Never can quite understand
The worth of a soul, and the change that's wrought
By the touch of the Master's hand.

2.   Editing your work is not as hard as revising. Part of editing is making sure you have no grammar, spelling, or punctuation errors. This will require a lot of concentration and care about details. You may want to proofread several times. Again, your teacher will be able to help you, but try to proofread your work first and catch as many errors as you can before you ask for your teacher's help. Proofread some of your work looking for any grammar, spelling, or punctuation errors. A grammar book and a dictionary will be useful for reference.

4.
1) A simile gives an idea or image of something by comparing it to something else using the word *like* or *as*.
2) A metaphor is a comparison in which one thing is said to be another.
3) Personification is comparing an object to a living thing.
4) Answers will vary.
5) The pattern in which a poem rhymes.
6) The use of stressed and unstressed syllables
7) Refer to Lesson 9, 1.
8) Refer to Lesson 9, 2.

3. Continue revising and editing the poems you have written during this unit. Begin making a neat copy of your completed work.

4. Take the time to review the lessons in this unit. Answer the following questions:

    1) What is a simile?
    2) What is a metaphor?
    3) What is personification?
    4) Give an example of each.
    5) Explain the rhyme scheme of a poem.
    6) Define feet.
    7) What is the importance of revisions?
    8) What does editing entail?

5. Finish the unit by:
    1) Reading aloud and discussing your poems and any other poems of your choice.
    2) Make a booklet containing your poems. You may wish to illustrate them.

Checklist for Poetry Booklet

☐ All poems neatly copied (Illustrations optional)
☐ Table of Contents completed
☐ Title page completed
☐ Cover illustrated and glued onto a folder
☐ Assembled in order
☐ Share with family and friends

---

    3) Recite the poem(s) you memorized this week.

Assessment 2
(Lessons 4 - 9)

1. Is the following a simile or a metaphor?

   Thy word is like honey.

2. Give an example of personification.

3. What is the rhyme scheme of the following poem?

Ring Out, Wild Bells by Alfred Tennyson

Ring out, wild bells, to the wild sky,
The flying cloud, the frosty light;
The year is dying in the night;
Ring out, wild bells, and let him die.

Ring out the old, ring in the new,
Ring, happy bells, across the snow;
The year is going, let him go;
Ring out the false, ring in the true.

1. It is a simile because it uses the word <u>like</u> to make the comparison.

2. Personification is a figure of speech in which an animal or inanimate object is given human characteristics.
   Ex: The sun smiled down upon our picnic.

3. The rhyme scheme is abba.

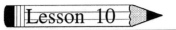

Lesson 10

The Borrowers

Teacher's Note: As your student completes this lesson, choose skills from the *Review Activties* that he needs. The *Review Activities* follow this lesson.

Mary Norton (1903 -) says the idea for the book came from an early fantasy in her childhood. Being a very nearsighted child she had to closely peer at objects in order to see them. On country walks with her brothers, she was a sore trial to them because of her habit of frequently stopping to gaze into every hedgerow, shallow pool, and ditch and wonder what life would be like for a small, vulnerable creature in those environments.

During times of childhood illness she would bring her "little people" indoors. "It was exciting to imagine there were others in the house, unguessed at by the adult humans who were living so close."

The Borrowers was awarded the Lewis Carroll Award in 1960.

Arrietty wandered through the open door into the sitting room. Ah, the fire had been lighted. The room looked bright and cozy. Homily was proud of her sitting room. The walls had been papered with scraps of old letters out of waste-paper baskets, and Homily had arranged the handwriting sideways in vertical stripes which ran from floor to ceiling. On the walls, repeated in various colors, hung several portraits of Queen Victoria as a girl. These were postage stamps.

The Borrowers by Mary Norton

1. a. Take the literature passage from dictation. Proofread, looking for any spelling or punctuation errors.

    b. Make a spelling list to study this week or use the following suggested list: wandered, ceiling, vertical, portraits.

    If you are unsure about how to spell **ie** or **ei** words, say each word aloud. Words are usually spelled with **ie**, but when it comes after **c**, use **ei**. If the word says the long /**a**/ sound, use **ei**.

    > **Spelling Tip**
    > i before e, except after c, and in words that say /a/ as in **neighbor** and **weigh**.

    c. Write the following words and underline **ie** and **ei**. Say the words aloud as you write them.

ie	cei	ei /ā/
pier	ceiling	reign
sieve	receive	eight
brief	receipt	heir
lien	deceive	neighbor
friend	deceit	weigh

d. Write **N** (Noun), **V**(Verb), **Pro** (Pronoun), or **Adj** (Adjective), above every word in the following sentences. Label articles and possessive nouns as adjectives.

1) The tired, old man rested.
2) He opened Jason's closet.

e. Look at the second sentence of the literature passage. The first word, *Ah,* is separated from the rest of the sentence with a comma. The word *ah* is a part of speech called an interjection. An **interjection** is a word or group of words which show strong or sudden feeling. Interjections may be separated with a comma (**,**) or an exclamation mark (**!**).

Ex: Ah! The fire had been lighted. *The* is capitalized because it begins a new sentence.

Ah, the fire had been lighted. The word *the* is not capitalized because it is not the first word in the sentence.

List of Common Interjections		
oh dear	well	wow
hey	ah	oh
my	yes	no

f. Write one sentence using an interjection separated with a comma; write another sentence using an interjection separated with an exclamation mark.

g. Look at the second sentence in the literature passage. Write the part of speech above each word: **N** (Noun), **V** (Verb), **Int** (Interjection), **Adj** (Adjective)

1.

  Adj Adj Adj   N
d.1) **The tired, old man**
         V
rested.
     Pro   V   Adj
  2) **He opened Jason's**
        N
closet.

f. Answers will vary.

 Int Adj   N   V   V
g. Ah, the fire had been
            V
lighted.

2. a. Say the word *admit* aloud. Can you hear the accent (stress) on the last syllable *mit*? **Accent** is where you put the stress in your voice when you say the word. Now, say *cover.* Can you hear the accent (stress) on the first syllable *cov*? If a two-syllable word is accented on the last syllable, follow the *Spelling Tip* below.

> **Spelling Tip**
> If a word has more than one syllable, ends with one vowel and one consonant, and the accent is on the last syllable, double the last consonant before adding a suffix beginning with a vowel.

Therefore, words like *wandered* which is accented on the first syllable, would not be spelled with a double **r**.
Ex: omit - omitted (the accent is on the last syllable)
      wander - wandered (the accent is on the first syllable)

b. Add the suffix. Say the words aloud as you write them.

	-ed	-ing
Ex:(accent on first syllable) wander	wandered	wandering
Ex:(accent on last syllable) omit	omitted	omitting

1) surrender
2) acquit
3) submit
4) pester
5) shower
6) transmit

c. You will remember that sentences have two main parts: the complete subject and the complete predicate. The simple subject is a noun or a pronoun and the simple predicate is a verb.

Underline the simple subject in the first sentence of the literature passage. Underline the verb twice.

2.
b.

-ed	-ing
1) surrendered	surrendering
2) acquitted	acquitting
3) submitted	submitting
4) pestered	pestering
5) showered	showering
6) transmitted	transmitting

2.
c. <u>Arietty</u> (simple subject); <u>wandered</u> (verb)

The usual English sentence pattern is the subject followed by verb. The next to the last sentence in the literature passage does not follow this order, so it may be harder for you to identify the subject.

d. Underline the subject *portraits*. Now, rewrite the sentence so that it follows the subject first pattern.

e. As you have learned earlier, a verb may consist of more than one verb. This is called a verb phrase. A verb phrase contains one main verb and one or more helping verbs. Being verbs are often used as helping verbs.
Ex: has been, should be, may have been, etc.

Common Helping Verbs				
have	do	shall	may	can
has	does	will	might	could
had	did	should	must	would

f. Using the literature passage, underline the helping verbs.

g. Using the following sentences, circle all the personal pronouns. Write the sentences again, replacing the pronouns with nouns.

1) They were rich.
2) He has been ill.
3) John received a gift from him.

3. a. Look at the literature passage, and circle all the action verbs.

The third sentence in the literature passage uses the verb, *looked*. Although *looked* is often used as an action verb, it can act as a special kind of verb called a linking verb. A linking verb does not show action but connects (or links) the subject with a word in the predicate. A **linking verb** is a verb which connects the subject to a word in the predicate.

2.

d. Possible answer: Repeated in various colors, several portraits of Queen Victoria as a girl hung on the walls.

f. <u>had</u> been lighted, <u>had</u> been papered, <u>had</u> arranged

g.1) (They) were rich.
   2) (He) has been ill.
   3) John received a gift from (him).
   Possible answers:
   1) John and Mary were rich.
   2) John has been ill.
   3) John received a gift from William.

3.

a. wandered, lighted, papered, arranged, ran, repeated, hung

List of Common Linking Verbs			
taste	feel	smell	sound
appear	become	seem	grow

Being verbs may also be linking verbs.

Being Verbs			
am	is	are	was
were	be	being	been

b. Look at the third sentence in the literature passage again. You have already determined that the word *looked* is a linking verb. It links the subject, *room*, to the adjectives in the predicate, *bright* and *cozy*. *Bright and cozy room* makes sense. *Bright* and *cozy* are called predicate adjectives. A **predicate adjective** will always be an adjective in the predicate describing the subject.

c. Underline the linking verbs in the following sentences. Draw an arrow from the adjective in the predicate to the word in the subject which it describes.

Ex: My father is brave.
The verb *is* links *father* to the adjective, *brave*.
Brave describes *father*. *Brave father* makes sense.

1) The pie tastes delicious.
2) My brother is kind.
3) The dinner smells burnt.
4) My friends were late.
5) My new pillow feels soft.

d. Now, look at the last sentence of the literature passage. *Were* in this sentence is a linking verb. It links the subject, *these* (portraits) to the noun in the predicate, *postage stamps*. *Postage stamps* is called a predicate nominative. A **predicate nominative** will always be a noun or pronoun in the predicate renaming the subject.

3.
c.
1) The pie <u>tastes</u> delicious.

2) My brother <u>is</u> kind.

3) The dinner <u>smells</u> burnt.

4) My friends <u>were</u> late.

5) My new pillow <u>feels</u> soft.

e. Underline the linking verbs in the following sentences. Draw an arrow from the noun in the predicate to the word in the subject which it renames.

Ex: My father is a brave man.
The verb *is* links *father* to the noun, *man*.
Man renames *father*. *Father is man* makes sense.

1) New Zealand is a beautiful country.
2) Benjamin Franklin was a great inventor.
3) The stray cat is a menace.
4) Paul quickly became my best friend.
5) Davis is the winner.

f. Review your spelling words.

4. a. Diagram only the subject and verb (or verb phrase) of the first three sentences of the literature passage.

b. Review Lesson 3, **4a** to see how you diagram the subject, verb, and adjectives. Locate the subject, verb, and adjectives in the following sentence. Diagram every word in the sentence.

The shaggy, old dog barked.

c. Look at the third sentence of the literature passage. What kind of verb is it?

d. Look at the fourth sentence of the literature passage. What kind of a verb is that?

e. Optional: Take an oral or written spelling pretest.

5. a. Take the literature passage from dictation.
OR
b. If you would like more practice with helping verbs, look for sentences in your easy-readers. Diagram the simple subjects and verb phrases.
OR
c. Write your own sentences and diagram them.
OR
d. Choose skills from the *Review Activities* on the next page.

3.
e.
1) New Zealand <u>is</u> a beautiful country.
2) Benjamin Franklin <u>was</u> a great inventor.
3) The stray cat <u>is</u> a menace.
4) Paul quickly <u>became</u> my best friend.
5) Davis <u>is</u> the winner.

4.
a.
1) Arrietty | wandered
2) fire | had been lighted
3) room | looked

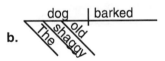
b.

c. linking verb

d. linking verb

1. Int V Pro V Adj
a. Wow! Did you see the
     Adj   N
   beautiful waterfall?
   Pro V   Adj   Adj
b. He painted his friend's
   N
   house.
   N   V   V   Adj
c. Samuel was calling his
   N
   sister.
  Int Pro V Adj   N
d. Hey, I saw ten elephants.
   N   V Adj Adj
e. Jan picked five ripe
   N
   tomatoes.

2.
a. taller
b. tallest
c. lovliest
d. more delightful

3. Possible answers:
a. Mr. Robert Simms
b. February
c. Presidents' Day
d. Yellowstone National Park
e. Australia

Review Activities

Choose the skills your student needs to review.

1. *Noun, Verb, Adjective, Pronoun, Interjection*
   Label the parts of speech. Label articles, possessive nouns, and possessive pronouns as adjectives: **N** (Noun), **V** (Verb), **Adj** (Adjective), **Pro** (Pronoun), **Int** (Interjection)

   a. Wow! Did you see the beautiful waterfall?
   b. He painted his friend's house.
   c. Samuel was calling his sister.
   d. Hey, I saw ten elephants.
   e. Jan picked five ripe tomatoes.

2. *Comparative and Superlative Adjectives*
   Use the comparative or superlative forms correctly.

   a. Philip is (*tall*) than Michael.
   b. Out of all his friends, Philip is (*tall*).
   c. Sue picked out the (*lovely*) dress of all.
   d. Visiting the Grand Canyon is (*delightful*) than I imagined.

3. *Common and Proper Nouns*
   Give a proper noun for the following common nouns.

   a. teacher
   b. month
   c. holiday
   d. park
   e. country

4. *Linking Verbs*
   Underline the linking verbs. Draw an arrow from the word in the predicate to the word in the subject which it describes or renames. Write if it is a predicate nominative (**PN**) or a predicate adjective (**PA**).

   a. The car is blue.
   b. Yesterday was sunny.
   c. The man seems strange.
   d. He is my brother.
   e. Jim was elected president.

5. *Diagram*
   Diagram only the subject, verb, and the adjective, which are bolded in the following sentences.

   a. **Your father is** late.
   b. **We were** rich then.
   c. **He has been** ill.

4.

a. The car <u>is</u> blue. (PA)

b. Yesterday <u>was</u> sunny. (PA)

c. The man <u>seems</u> strange. (PA)

d. He <u>is</u> my brother. (PN)

e. Jim <u>was</u> elected president. (PN)

5.

a.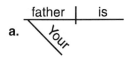

b. $\underline{\quad We \mid were \quad}$

c. $\underline{\quad He \mid has\ been \quad}$

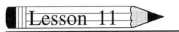

Teacher's Note: As your student completes this lesson, choose skills from the *Review Activties* that he needs. The *Review Activities* follow this lesson.

 *Homily knitted their jerseys and stockings on black-headed pins, and, sometimes, on darning needles. A great reel of silk or cotton would stand, table high, beside her chair, and sometimes, if she pulled too sharply, the reel would tip up and roll away out of the open door into the dusty passage beyond, and Arrietty would be sent after it, to re-wind it carefully as she rolled it back.*

The Borrowers by Mary Norton

1. a. Take the literature passage from dictation. Proofread, looking for any spelling or punctuation errors.

   b. Make a spelling list to study this week or use the following suggested list: jerseys, stockings, cotton, passage.

   If a the word ends with a single short vowel and the **/k/** sound, it will often be spelled **ck**.

   > ### Spelling Tip
   > In most words, a **/k/** sound will be spelled **ck** if it follows a single short vowel.

   c. Circle the correctly spelled word.

1) money is kept here	banck	bank
2) black liquid for writing	ink	inck
3) opposite of float	sink	sinck
4) to create	macke	make
5) a water bird	duk	duck
6) a piece	chunk	chunck
7) you wear on your foot	sok	sock
8) to gather leaves	rake	racke

   d. How did you do with the commas in your dictation? This paragraph contains many commas to help the reader understand what the author is trying to say.

   There are some basic rules for comma usage (which you will be learning), but authors may also use it to add clarity to an unusually long sentence.

1.
c. 1) banck (bank)
2) (ink) inck
3) (sink) sinck
4) macke (make)
5) duk (duck)
6) (chunk) chunck
7) sok (sock)
8) (rake) racke

e. Look at the following sentence:

Homily knitted their jerseys and stockings.

Circle the word *and.* What two words do they join?

The word *and* is a conjunction. The term conjunction comes from the Latin word *con,* which means *together*; and *jungere* which means *join.* Therefore, a **conjunction** is a word that joins words, groups of words, or simple sentences together. Look at the following list of common conjunctions.

List of Common Conjunctions

and	but	or	so

f. Circle all the conjunctions in the literature passage.

g. As you have already noticed, the second sentence in the literature passage is very long, connected with several commas and conjunctions. Make some minor changes and divide it into two or three sentences instead of one long one. There are many different ways to write the sentences. Remember, each sentence must have a subject and predicate.

2. a. Before you change a word ending in **y** into its plural form, look at the word. If the word ends with a vowel and **y,** just add **s.** If the word ends with a consonant and **y,** change the **y** to **i** and add **es.**

Spelling Tip
To form the plural of words ending with **y** preceded by a vowel, just add **s.** To form the plural of words ending with **y** preceded by a consonant, change the **y** to **i** and add **es.**

1.
e. jerseys, stockings

f. and, and, or, and, and, and

g. Possible answer:
A great reel of silk or cotton would stand, table high, beside her chair. Sometimes, if she pulled too sharply, the reel would tip up and roll way out of the open door into the dusty passage beyond. Arrietty would be sent after it, to re-wind it carefully as she rolled it back.

73

2.

b. Ends with vowel and y - just add s
1) monkeys
2) turkeys
3) attorneys
4) donkeys
5) alleys

Ends with consonant and y - change y to i and add es
6) supplies
7) pansies
8) communities
9) academies
10) parties

d. knitted

e. Homily knitted yesterday.

g. Past / Past Participle
1) wandered (have) wandered
2) looked (have) looked
3) arranged (have) arranged
4) repeated (have) repeated
5) rolled (have) rolled

b. Write the plural form for the following words:

Ends with vowel and y Just add s	Ends with consonant and y Change y to i and add es
Ex: jersey jerseys	
Ex: poppy	poppies

1) monkey
2) turkey
3) attorney
4) donkey
5) alley
6) supply
7) pansy
8) community
9) academy
10) party

c. A verb has several different forms because it expresses different times. The Latin word for time is *tense*. Without **verb tenses** we wouldn't be able to tell if something happened yesterday, is happening today, or will happen tomorrow.

d. Look at the first sentence in the literature passage. What is the verb?

e. Does the sentence tell you Homily *knits today, knitted yesterday,* or *will knit tomorrow?*

f. Verbs have three basic forms. These forms are called the principal parts of the verb. They are the present, past, and past participle.

g. Fill in the chart correctly.

Present	Past	Past Participle
Ex: knit	knitted	(have) knitted
1) wander		
2) look		
3) arrange		
4) repeat		
5) roll		

h. Read the following sentence aloud.

Marty read a story out of the red book.

There are two words which sound the same but are spelled differently and have different meanings. Words like *read* and *red* are called homonyms. **Homonyms** are words that sound the same, have a different meaning and usually have a different spelling.

i. Read the literature passage carefully again and list all the homonyms.

3. a. Before you change a word ending in **o** into its plural form, look at the word. If the word ends with a vowel and **o**, just add **s**. If the word ends with a consonant and **o**, add **es**. Words that relate to music always form their plural form by just adding **s**.

> ### Spelling Tip
> To form the plural of words ending in **o** preceded by a consonant, add **es.** To form the plural of words ending in **o** preceded by a vowel, just add **s.** Musical words are exceptions; they always form plurals by just adding **s.**

b. Write the following words in the plural form.

	o preceded by a consonant Add es	o preceded by a vowel Just add s	musical words Just add s
Ex: studio		studios	
Ex: potato	potatoes		
Ex: banjo			banjos
1) hero			
2) tomato			
3) rodeo			
4) piano			
5) soprano			
6) echo			
7) trio			

✏ **Teacher's Note: Some grammar books teach this as a homophone.**

2.
i. their (there, they're)
   great (grate)
   reel (real)
   would (wood)
   high (hi)
   too (to, two)
   roll (role)
   be (bee)
   sent (scent, cent)

3.
b. O preceded by a consonant add es
   1) heroes
   2) tomatoes
   6) echoes

O preceded by a vowel just add s
   3) rodeos

just add s
   4) pianos
   5) sopranos
   7) trios

3. c. The past and past participle were formed by adding -ed to the present tense.

d. Past   Past Participle
1) ran   (have) run
2) sat   (have) sat
3) stood   (have) stood
4) sent   (have) sent
5) wound   (have) wound
6) sang   (have) sung
7) swam   (have) swam

e. knitted (R)
   would stand (IR)
   pulled (R)
   would tip (R)
   roll (R)
   would be sent (IR)

4. a. Homily knits their jerseys and stockings on black-headed pins, and sometimes, on darning needles. A great reel of silk or cotton stands table high, beside her chair, and sometimes, if she pulls too sharply, the reel tips up and rolls away out of the open door into the dusty passage beyond, (and Arrietty will be sent after it, to re-wind it carefully as she rolls it back.)

b. Arriety wanders through the open door into the sitting room. Ah, the fire is lit. The room looks bright and cozy. Homily is proud of her sitting room. The walls are papered with scraps of old letters out of waste-paper baskets, and Homily arranges the handwriting sideways in vertical stripes which run from floor to ciling. On the walls, repeated in various colors, hang several portraits of Queen Victoria as a girl. These are postage stamps.

c. Look at the verbs you worked with yesterday. How were most of the past and past participle verbs formed?

These are called **regular verbs** because the past and past participle forms are made by adding **-ed** to the present form.

Many verbs do not follow this regular way of forming principal parts, as in the case of *hung*. Therefore, they are called **irregular verbs**. The following chart contains some common irregular verbs. There are many more irregular verbs.

d. Fill in the chart.

Present	**Past**	**Past Participle**
Ex: hang	hung	(have) hung
1) run		
2) sit		
3) stand		
4) send		
5) wind		
6) sing		
7) swim		

e. Underline the verbs in the literature passage. Circle the helping verbs. Indicate if they are regular (**R**) or irregular verbs (**IR**). Omit the last phrase in the passage beginning "to rewind...back."

f. Review your spelling words.

4. a. Rewrite the literature passage in the present tense.

b. For more practice with verb tenses, rewrite the literature passage from Lesson 10 in the present tense also.

c. Optional: Take an oral or written spelling pretest.

5. a. Take the literature passage from dictation.
                    OR
b. Using your easy-readers, find five verbs and write their three principal parts.
                    OR
c. Choose skills from the *Review Activities* on the next page.

Review Activities

Choose the skills your student needs to review.

1. *Noun, Verb, Adjective, Pronoun, Conjunction*
   Label the parts of speech in the following sentences. Label articles and possessive pronouns as adjectives. **N** (Noun), **V** (Verb), **Adj** (Adjective), **Pro** (Pronoun), **Conj** (Conjunction)

   a. Todd cleaned the dirty house.
   b. It took a long time.
   c. Little creatures filled the dark forest.
   d. Ron brought his mother and father.
   e. Sal thought his friend had called him.

2. *Subject / Verb / Adjective / Noun*
   Using the following sentences underline the subject once and underline the verb twice. Draw an arrow from the adjective (including article and possessive pronoun) to the noun it describes.

   a. The hungry boy ate his lunch.
   b. Yesterday, I visited my best friend.
   c. Jonathan leaped over the broken fence.
   d. Marla sang a lovely song.
   e. We found a lost dog.

1.
a. Todd cleaned the dirty house.
   N   V   Adj Adj N

b. It took a long time.
   Pro V Adj Adj N

c. Little creatures filled the dark forest.
   Adj   N   V   Adj N

d. Ron brought his mother and father.
   N   V   Adj   N   Conj N

e. Sal thought his friend had called him.
   N   V   Adj   N   V   V   Pro

2.
a. The hungry boy ate his lunch.

b. Yesterday, I visited my best friend.

c. Jonathan leaped over the broken fence.

d. Marla sang a lovely song.

e. We found a lost dog.

3.

a.
```
  puppy  | escaped
\The \timid
```

b.
```
   car   | groaned
\The \old
```

c.
```
  sister | laughed
\My
```

d.
```
  puppies | whimpered
\Six \little
```

e.
```
  brother | came
\Sara's
```

4.

Past	Past Participle
a. wanted	(have) wanted
b. went	(have) gone
c. wrote	(have) written
d. screamed	(have) screamed
e. flew	(have) flown
f. looked	(have) looked
g. cleaned	(have) cleaned
h. talked	(have) talked
i. stole	(have) stolen
j. ordered	(have) ordered

3. _Diagram - Subject, Verb, Adjective_
Diagram each (subject, verb, and adjective) word in every sentence.

a. The timid puppy escaped.
b. The old car groaned.
c. My sister laughed.
d. Six little puppies whimpered.
e. Sara's brother came.

4. _Verb Tense (Regular and Irregular)_
Fill in the chart.

Present	Past	Past Participle
a. want		
b. go		
c. write		
d. scream		
e. fly		
f. look		
g. clean		
h. talk		
i. steal		
j. order		

"Your mother and I got you up," said Pod, "to tell you about upstairs."
Arrietty, holding the great cup in both hands, looked at him over the edge. Pod coughed. "You said a while back that the sky was dark brown with cracks in it. Well, it isn't." He looked at her almost accusingly. "It's blue."
"I know," said Arrietty.
"You know!" exclaimed Pod.

The Borrowers by Mary Norton

Teacher's Note: As your student completes this lesson, choose skills from the *Review Activties* that he needs. The *Review Activities* follow this lesson.

1. a. Take the literature passage from dictation. Proofread, looking for any spelling or punctuation errors.

   b. Make a spelling list to study this week or use the following suggested list: coughed, accusingly, exclaimed, almost.

   Words like *cough* can be tough words to spell correctly. Try to remember the **/ff/** sound may sometimes be spelled **gh**.

   > **Spelling Tip**
   > The **/ff/** sound may be spelled with **gh**, as in *cough*.

   c. Write the following words, and underline **gh**. Say the words aloud as you write them.

cough	draught
tough	laugh
enough	rough

   d. How did you do with the punctuation in your dictation? Look at the first sentence of the literature passage. Read aloud the exact words spoken by Pod.

1.

d. Your mother and I got you up to tell you about upstairs. You said a while back that the sky was dark brown with cracks in it. Well it isn't. It's blue. You know!

Notice how the quotation is split by *said Pod*. Also, notice how it is punctuated and capitalized. This is a **split quotation**. Write a split quotation. Remember to place quotation marks only around the exact words spoken or thought.

For further information on quotation mark rules, look in Lesson 18, **1d**.

2. a. Before you write a word ending in **f** or **fe** in its plural form, say the plural word aloud. If you hear a **/f/** sound, just add **s**. If you hear a **/v/** sound, change the **f** to **v** and add **es**.

> ### Spelling Tip
> To form the plural of words ending in **f** and **fe**, say the plural word aloud. If you hear a **/f/** sound, just add **s**. If you hear a **/v/** sound, change the **f** to **v** and add **es**.

Ex: chief - Say the word as a plural aloud. /Cheefs/ You can hear the **/f/** sound, therefore, spell it **c-h-i-e-f-s**.

wife - Say the plural word aloud. /wivs/ You can hear the **/v/** sound, therefore, spell it **w-i-v-e-s**.

b. Write the plural form of the following words. It is helpful to say the plural word aloud.
   1) knife
   2) roof
   3) loaf
   4) hoof

c. Look at the first word of the literature passage. Do not confuse the possessive pronoun *your* with the contraction *you're*.
   Ex: Bring *your* books.
       You're going to need them for your book report.

2.
b. 1) knives
  2) roofs
  3) loaves
  4) hooves

Do not confuse the possessive pronoun *its* with the contraction *it's*.

Ex: *It's* funny watching the cat chase *its* tail.

Do not confuse the possessive pronoun *their* with the contraction *they're* or the commonly used word, *there*.

Ex: *There* is a large crowd at the symphony.
      They're very good.
      It was *their* best performance.

d. Complete the sentences with the correct word.
   1) Justin and Grace brought (*there, their, they're*) dog.
   2) (*There, Their, They're*) going on vacation.
   3) (*Its, It's*) time to walk the dog.
   4) The dog licked (*its, it's*) paw.
   5) Give me (*your, you're*) address.
   6) (*Your, You're*) going to get a postcard from me.

e. The basic building blocks of a sentence are a noun or pronoun as the subject, and a verb as the predicate. Therefore, we can write complete sentences that have only two words.

Ex: Billy ran.
          Birds fly.

Find two two-word sentences in the literature passage.

Note: "It's blue" is actually a three word sentence: "It is blue."

Diagram only the quotation.

f. Look at the fifth sentence of the literature passage. What part of speech is the word, *well?*

g. Do you remember why the comma is used after the word *well?*

2.
d. 1) their
   2) They're
   3) It's
   4) its
   5) your
   6) You're

e.   I | know

     You | know

f. Interjection

g. Interjections are set off with a comma or an exclamation mark.

3. a. You have learned how to form plurals for some words. Today, you will learn how to form plurals of special compound nouns. Place the **s** after the main part of the word.
Ex: brother-in-law
    brothers-in-law (correct)
    brother-in-laws (incorrect)

To form a plural possessive of compound nouns, just add apostrophe **s** (**'s**) at the end of the plural word.
Ex: brother-in-law's — singular possessive
     brothers-in-law's — plural possessive

> ## Spelling Tip
> To form a plural of a special compound word, add the **s** to the main part of the word. To form a plural possessive compound word, add the apostrophe **s** (**'s**) at the end of the word.

b. Complete the chart.

3.

b. Plural
  1) fathers-in-law
  2) secretaries-of-state
  3) chairmen-of- the-board

Plural Possessive
  4) fathers-in-law's
  5) secretaries-of-state's
  6) chairmen-of-the-board's

Singular	**Plural**
Ex: brother-in-law	brothers-in-law
1) father-in-law	
2) secretary-of-state	
3) chairman of the board	

Singular Possessive	**Plural Possessive**
Ex: brother-in-law's	brothers-in-law's
4) father-in-law's	
5) secretary-of-state's	
6) chairman-of-the-board's	

c. Some verbs work well in a two-word sentence. However, there are verbs that need another noun after them to make the sentence complete. For example, if we read *Jack caught,* we would need more information for the sentence to be complete. We want to know what Jack caught. A cold, a ball, a fish, or me? The verb *caught* transfers the action from Jack to the object he caught. The receiver of the action is called the **direct object**. Since the direct object receives the action of the verb, only action verbs will have direct objects. A verb that has a direct object is called a **transitive verb**.

d. In the first part of the sentence spoken by Pod, what is the
    direct object of the transitive verb *got*? You can find the
    direct object by asking the question, "Whom or what did Pod
    get?"

> **Hint**
>
> The direct object is **always** a
> noun or pronoun that answers
> *whom* or *what*.

3.
d. you

Many verbs are **not** transitive, which means they do not need
an object to complete their action. These verbs are called
intransitive verbs. Many verbs can be either transitive or
intransitive.

> **Hint**
>
> A verb that has a direct object
> is a transitive verb.

e. Underline the transitive verbs in the following sentences
    about *The Borrowers*. Circle its direct object. Remember,
    the direct object should answer the question *whom* or *what*
    after the verb and should be a noun or pronoun.
    Ex: John threw the ball.
        John threw *what*?
        John threw the *ball*.
        Ball is the direct object.

    1) She swept the passages.
    2) She had tidied her hair.
    3) She caught her breath.
    4) He lost his oars.

3.
e.1) She <u>swept</u> the
    (passages.) Swept
    what?
  2) She <u>had tidied</u> her (hair.)
    Had tidied what?
  3) She <u>caught</u> her (breath.)
    Caught what?
  4) He <u>lost</u> his (oars.) Lost
    what?

f. Since the direct object is a foundational part of a sentence, it
    is diagrammed on the same foundational line as the subject
    and verb. After the verb, draw a vertical line that does not
    cross the base line and add the direct object to the right of the
    new line. If the direct object has an adjective, add a diagonal
    line below the direct object.

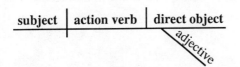

Ex: I wrote a letter.

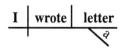

3.
g. 1)

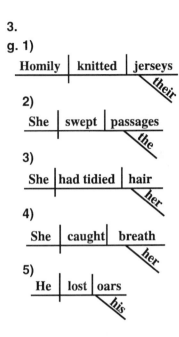

g. Diagram the subject, verb, adjective, and direct object in the following sentences. Every word will be diagrammed.
   1) Homily knitted their jerseys.
   2) She swept the passages.
   3) She had tidied her hair.
   4) She caught her breath.
   5) He lost his oars.

h. Look at the last sentence of the literature passage. By using the vivid word *exclaimed* instead of *said*, the sentence shows more feeling. These word are called **synonyms**. A **thesaurus** is a book of synonyms.

i. Possible answers:
   1) "Help me!" *cried* a voice in the crowd.
   2) "I am so relieved to see you," *sighed* Russell.
   3) Mark *yelled*, "Don't touch that!"
   4) Mom *warned*, "You must be back before dark."
   5) "I'm hungry," *whined* the toddler.

i. Replace the italicized words with synonyms which show more feeling.
   1) "Help me!" *said* a voice in the crowd.
   2) "I am so relieved to see you," *said* Russell.
   3) Mark *said*, "Don't touch that!"
   4) Mom *said*, "You must be back before dark."
   5) "I'm hungry," *said* the toddler.

j. Review your spelling words.

4. a. Some sentences with direct objects will also have an indirect object. Like the direct object, the **indirect object** is also a noun or pronoun that helps to complete the action begun by the subject and verb by answering the questions *to whom* or *for whom*. An indirect object never follows the words *to* or *for.*

Hint
The **indirect object** will always be a noun or pronoun that answers the question *to whom* or *for whom*.

> ## Hint
>
> If there is no direct object, there is no indirect object.

Ex: I <u>wrote</u> her a letter.
    I wrote *what*? I wrote a *letter*.
    The direct object is *letter*.

I wrote a letter *to whom*?
I wrote a letter to *her*.
The indirect object is *her*.

b. Underline the verb in each of these sentences about *The Borrowers*. Then circle the direct object and draw an arrow from the direct object to the indirect object.

Ex: I <u>wrote</u> her a (letter.)
1) Mrs. May taught her many things.
2) I will bring you some supper.
3) Pod had made her a hairbrush.

c. If a sentence has an indirect object, add a slanted line below the verb line with a line attached to it running parallel to the base line. The indirect object is written on the line parallel to the base line.

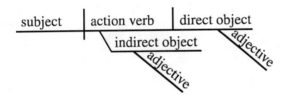

Ex: I wrote her mother a letter.

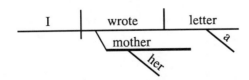

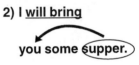

4.
b.1) Mrs. May <u>taught</u>

    her many (things.)

2) I <u>will bring</u>

    you some (supper.)

3) Pod <u>had made</u>

    her a (hairbrush.)

4.

d.

1)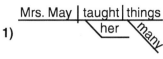

2)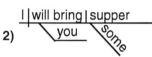

3)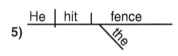

4)

5)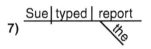

6)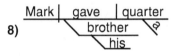

7) Sue | typed | report / the

8) Mark | gave | quarter / brother / his \ a

d. Diagram the subject, verb, adjective, direct object, and indirect object in the following sentences. Every word will be diagrammed.
   1) Mrs. May taught her many things.
   2) I will bring you some supper.
   3) Pod had made her a hairbrush.
   4) Bill sent his grandmother a letter.
   5) He hit the fence.
   6) The big dog licked my hand.
   7) Sue typed the report.
   8) Mark gave his brother a quarter.

e. Optional: Take an oral or written spelling pretest.

5. a. Take the literature passage from dictation.

                          OR

   b. Using your easy-readers, locate the subject, verb or verb phrase, direct object, and indirect object.

                          OR

   c. Choose skills from the *Review Activities* on the next page.

Review Activities

Choose the skills your student needs to review.

1. *Homonyms*
   Choose the correct word.

   a. Charlotte's face turned (*red, read*) as a (*beat, beet*).
   b. Mother gave everyone a (*peace, piece*) of pie.
   c. Russell accomplished a great (*feet, feat*) when he ran the race.
   d. My voice is (*horse, hoarse*) from screaming at the football game.
   e. The bread is very dry and (*course, coarse*).

2. *Capitalization and Punctuation*
   Capitalize and punctuate.

   a. next thursday said mr wilcox we will dissect a frog
   b. aunt marsha moved into our house on yardley avenue
   c. karen carefully unpacked four crystal ornaments and placed them on her grandmothers hutch
   d. jack asked may I go with mark chuck and jill
   e. excuse me interrupted carl but I need to speak to you

3. *Transitive Verb and Direct Object*
   Underline the transitive verb and circle the direct object.

   a. I ate an apple for dessert.
   b. Steve delivers newspapers.
   c. She read a book.
   d. Chris and I climbed a mountain.
   e. The spider spun a beautiful web.

1.
a. red beet
b. piece
c. feat
d. hoarse
e. coarse

2.
a. "Next Thursday," said Mr. Wilcox, "we will dissect a frog."
b. Aunt Marsha moved into our house on Yardley Avenue.
c. Karen carefully unpacked four crystal ornaments and placed them on her grandmother's hutch.
d. Jack asked, "May I go with Mark, Chuck, and Jill?"
e. "Excuse me," interrupted Carl, "but I need to speak to you."

3.
a. I <u>ate</u> an (apple) for dessert.
b. Steve <u>delivers</u> (newspapers.)
c. She <u>read</u> a (book.)
d. Chris and I <u>climbed</u> a (mountain.)
e. The spider <u>spun</u> a beautiful (web.)

4. Possible answers:

a. strolled, meandered, paced

b. hollered, screamed, called

c. humorous, comical, hilarious

d. weird, unusual, mysterious

e. peered, gazed, stared

5.

a. The shepherd carried the <u>lamb</u>.

b. We sang many <u>songs</u>.

c. Jenny lost her <u>ring</u>.

d. I read (him) a funny <u>story</u>.

e. Robert drew (her) a detailed <u>map</u>.

f. It taught (him) a good <u>lesson</u>.

g. They baked (her) a delicious <u>cake</u>.

h. I asked (him) <u>permission</u>.

6.

a. shepherd | carried | lamb / The \ the

b. We | sang | songs \ many

c. Jenny | lost | ring \ her

d. I | read | story \ him \ a \ funny

e. Robert | drew | map \ her \ a \ detailed

f. It | taught | lesson \ him \ a \ good

g. They | baked | cake \ her \ a \ delicious

h. I | asked | permission \ him

4. *Synonyms*
Write a synonym for the following words.

a. walked
b. yelled
c. funny
d. strange
e. looked

5. *Direct Object and Indirect Object*
Underline the direct object and circle the indirect object.

a. The shepherd carried the lamb.
b. We sang many songs.
c. Jenny lost her ring.
d. I read him a funny story.
e. Robert drew her a detailed map.
f. It taught him a good lesson.
g. They baked her a delicious cake.
h. I asked him permission.

6. *Diagram (Subject, Verb, Direct Object, Indirect Object, Adjective)*
Diagram the sentences in **5a-h**. Diagram every word in each sentence.

Assessment 3
(Lessons 10 - 12)

1. Underline the subject once and underline the action verbs twice in the following sentences:

    a. The storm tossed the ship.
    b. The men cried out in fear.
    c. The Savior woke up.
    d. He calmed the storm.
    e. The men worshipped Him.

2. Which of the verbs you underlined are regular? Which are irregular?

3. List the different forms of the verb *be*.

4. Underline the verb phrase in the following sentence. Circle the helping verb.

    We are going with him.

5. Diagram only the subject and verb in the above sentence. Not every word will be diagrammed.

6. Rewrite the sentences in **1a - e** changing the verbs to the present tense.

7. Give an example of a transitive verb.

8. Underline the direct object in the following sentences:

    a. The young boy threw the paper.
    b. I fed the dog.
    c. Sam found his green jacket.

1.
a. The <u>storm</u> <u>tossed</u> the ship.
b. The <u>men</u> <u>cried</u> out in fear.
c. The <u>Savior</u> <u>woke</u> up.
d. <u>He</u> <u>calmed</u> the storm.
e. The <u>men</u> <u>worshipped</u> Him.

2.
a. tossed - regular
b. cried - regular
c. woke - irregular
d. calmed - regular
e. worshipped - regular

3. be, being, been, am, is, are, was, were

4. We (are) going with him.

5. <u>We | are going</u>

6.
a. The storm *tosses* the ship.
b. The men *cry* out in fear.
c. The Savior *wakes* up.
d. He *calms* the storm.
e. The men *worship* Him.

7. Possible answers: make, feed, cut

8.
a. The young boy threw the <u>paper</u>.
b. I fed the <u>dog</u>.
c. Sam found his green <u>jacket</u>.

9.

a.
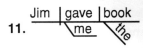
boy | threw | paper
The young   the

b.
I | fed | dog
        the

c.
Sam | found | jacket
          his green

10. Jim gave (me) the **book**.

11.
Jim | gave | book
      me   the

9. Diagram the subject, verb, adjective, and direct object in the sentences in **8a-c**. Every word will be diagrammed.

10. Underline the direct object in the following sentence and circle the indirect object.

   Jim gave me the book.

11. Diagram the above sentence.

BOOK STUDY

on
Star of Light

Star of Light
by Patricia St. John
Published by Moody Press

Readability level: 7ᵗʰ Grade

Patricia St. John (1919-1993) was an English author who spent over 25 years of her life as a missionary in the Mid-East. Her first book, *Tanglewood Secrets*, was published in 1940 and in 1983 she received the Children's Book Award for *Nothing Else Matters*.

Star of Light tells of her own experiences as a missionary in Tangier, Morocco. She spent her last years in England serving as president of Global Care, a foundation that helps children in impoverished nations.

Summary

Star of Light tells the story of Hamid and Jenny, two children from two very different worlds, whose lives are changed through the ministry of a missionary nurse. Out of necessity, Hamid's mother has become the number two wife of a cruel and greedy man. They are a people who worship idols and live in fear of evil spirits.

Hamid is a loving son and brother who is saddened to learn that his beloved baby sister, Kinza, is blind. When his stepfather learns of this, he makes arrangements to hire Kinza out as a beggar and eventually decides to sell her to the beggar.

Remembering a kind missionary nurse who had once befriended her, Hamid's mother entrusts him with taking Kinza to the nurse where she knows she will be well cared for. After a tiring journey full of adventure, Hamid comes to the nurse's house and leaves Kinza on her doorstep. He returns to Bible classes taught by the nurse in order to receive food and also to keep an eye on Kinza.

Many miles away, a much spoiled and petted little girl, Jenny, is recovering from a serious illness. Her parents have been advised to take her away to a warmer climate. Her mother remembers her old friend, known to Jenny as "Aunt" Rosemary, and it is decided to visit her in Northern Africa. Jenny is charmed by Aunt Rosemary's adopted blind child and immediately wants to help Aunt Rosemary in her work. As she serves alongside her aunt she begins to sense that something is missing from her own life.

The climax of the story is reached when Kinza's stepfather kidnaps her, and Aunt Rosemary and Hamid rush to her rescue. Hamid and Jenny find the answer to the hunger they feel in their hearts. Written by a former missionary, Patricia St. John, this story is about true events and people she has known.

Discussion Questions and Activities

Chapters 1-9

1. a. Read the Introductory Note in *Star of Light*. Look at a map and find out where this story might have taken place.

    b. Read Chapters 1-3.

    c. Contrast the way women, children, and marriage are treated in Hamid's country with ways they are treated in our country. To **contrast** is to stress the differences. Your essay should contain **transitional words** such as *on the other hand, however, but, on the contrary, as opposed, counter to,* etc.

    You will not be spending a lot of time researching this topic, so the essay could be just a couple of paragraphs. The following is a sample essay:

    In Hamid's country women and children are treated very differently than they are in the United States. There they are looked down upon, made to carry heavy loads, and work a full twelve hour day. As opposed to the United States where children are usually in school and women, if they work outside the home, have much shorter hours. Women in the United States are treated more as equals to men counter to Hamid's country where they are looked upon as property to be used.

    Marriage is also seen much differently in Hamid's country. For instance, polygamy, the practice of having more than one wife, is common. On the contrary, in the United States polygamy is illegal. Also, Hamid's mother married a man because she does not have any means of supporting herself and her children. He married her because of the free labor she and her children will give him. On the other hand, people in the United States usually marry for love, not giving much thought to financial matters.

    d. Optional: Research blindness or read a biography of Helen Keller, Fanny Crosby, or Louis Braille. A **biography** is a true story written about someone by somebody else.

2.   Read Chapters 4-6. Try retelling this portion of the story in your own words. This is called **narration**.

3. a. Storytellers tell their stories in three voices:

   - First person
     First person is when the story is told by a character in the story as if he were talking directly to you telling the story through his eyes. The pronoun *I* is used.

   - Second person
     Second person does not lend itself to storytelling and is rarely used. If you have ever read the *Choose Your Own Adventure* stories, you will notice that these are told in the second person and you, the reader, are directly addressed.

   - Third person
     Third person is when the story is being told by someone outside the story, as if they had observed it and now are telling you what happened.

   b. Stories are usually told in the first and third person. In what voice is *Star of Light* told?

   c. Chapters 1-6 introduced four main characters.

   Hamid
   Hamid's sister, Kinza
   Kinza's mother
   Kinza's stepfather

   During the next three days you will be writing a **character sketch** of these main characters. You will be writing a short paper describing each character.

   To write an effective character sketch, be sure to include the character's personal as well as physical characteristics.

3.
b. *Star of Light* is written in the third person.

Some physical characteristics to consider:
- What does she look like?
- How does she carry herself?
- What kind of clothes is she wearing?
- How does she speak?

Some personal characteristics to consider:
- What is important to him?
- Is he friendly? Shy? Intelligent?
- What are his thoughts?

Today, write from Hamid's **point of view**, using the first person, as if you were the character. Tell how he feels about his sister and family and their situation. Tell of his problems and concerns as if you were Hamid.

The following is a sample character sketch of Hamid. There is no right or wrong way to do this.

My name is Hamid. I am eleven years old and I live in a country in Africa. I am the oldest in my family. I have a nine-year-old sister, Rahma, and a two-year-old sister, Kinza. My father died when I was nine years old and my mother married a man named Si Mohamed because she couldn't feed all of us by herself. Si Mohamed's older wife is very mean to my poor mother, my sisters, and me. I work hard each day taking care of his goats.

My dear little sister, Kinza, is blind. In my country blind people are not considered useful. I knew Si Mohamed would be angry when he found out and would want to give Kinza away. The night when he found out he was surprisingly calm. He said that when Kinza was old enough she could beg. I was angry. I did not want my little sister to become a beggar! When she was two years old Si Mohamed took her to the village to beg. I love my little sister so much. My mother has come up with a way for me to save Kinza. I am very proud of her trust in me and have pledged myself to protect and guide Kinza all her life.

Now go back and review the information given about Kinza and write a character sketch of her in the first person. Tell how she feels about her family and situation.

The following is a sample character sketch of Kinza:

Kinza is my name. It means "treasure." That is how my big brother Hamid treats me. He gently carries me because I am not very strong. I love to sit in the sun and feel its warmth, even if I can't see its light. I cannot see my mother's face either, but I love her soft touch. I also love to listen for Hamid's footsteps. I feel safest when I am cradled in his arms.

I am usually very happy, except on market days. Then my stepfather makes Hamid carry me to the village to beg. It is a noisy and dirty place. The flies and fleas torment me, but worst of all, Hamid must leave me alone there with the old beggar. He is not kind to me. If I fall asleep in the long, hot afternoon, he slaps me to wake me up and curses at me. When my stepfather agreed to sell me to the beggar and his wife, my mother decided I must go away with Hamid. I am not sure where we are going, but I know Hamid will take care of me.

4. a. Describe Kinza's mother's life as if you were her. How would you feel if you were Hamid's mother? Scan over what you have read. Look for insights into understanding Hamid's mother.

   b. Finally, and this might be the hardest to do, create a character sketch of Hamid's stepfather from the first person. How do you think he thinks and feels? Again, you will probably have to scan over the material you have read.

These character sketches will follow Day 3's pattern.

4.
a. Answers will vary.

b. Answers will vary.

5. a. Read Chapter 7 "A Narrow Escape." Narrate the chapter back to your teacher with as much detail as you remember.

Using information found in Chapters 6 and 7, draw an imaginary map of Hamid's and Kinza's journey. Include the places mentioned and label them.

The map might look something like this:

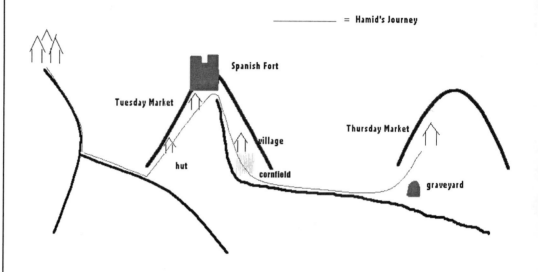

b. Read Chapters 8 and 9.

Chapters 10-17

1. a. Read Chapters 10-12 silently.

   b. Read Chapter 11 out loud to your teacher. Use good expression and speak clearly.

2. a. In chapter 11, the English nurse uses Hamid's deception as an opportunity to teach him about walking in the light and being clean. She does this by making an analogy. An **analogy** is the comparison of unfamiliar ideas with something that is simple or more familiar.

   b. What are some analogies that Jesus made in Scripture?

   c. Today you will begin writing an analogy. First think of what you would like to explain. Then write a story that illustrates this spiritual lesson.

   The following familiar story is an example of this kind of analogy:

   One day a boy carved a beautiful little boat out of a block of wood. He eagerly took the boat to a nearby lake and placed it upon the water. A strong wind blew his boat far out in the lake, too far for the boy to reach it. Sadly, the little boy had to go home without his boat.

   Months went by and one day the little boy was walking down the main street of the town. He happened to pass a store that sold trinkets and odd items. Imagine the boy's joy as he looked in the window and saw his little boat for sale!

   He rushed home, broke open his piggybank, and taking all of his money, he ran back to the store to buy his boat. As the little boy left the shop, he cradled his precious boat in his arms and said, "Now you are twice mine. Once because I made you, and once because I bought you for a price."

2.
b. **Allow time for discussion.**

3.
b. Refer to your map.

4.
a. Allow time for
   discussion.

3. a. Read Chapters 13-14.
   A new character, Jenny Swift, has been introduced. Write a character sketch of Jenny as you did of the other main characters. Follow the pattern as directed in Lesson 13, **3c**.

   b. Look at a map and find the probable route taken by Jenny and her family from England to North Africa.

4. a. Read Chapters 15-17.
   Discuss Jenny's statement at the end of Chapter 16: "If only Kinza could come back," said Jenny to herself, "I would never be disobedient or naughty again. I'd be good for ever and ever."

   b. Today, find some facts about the Islam religion.
   Use the encyclopedia or library books. As you read, list some major beliefs and practices. What is its origin?

5. a. Using the information you gathered yesterday, along with what you know about Christianity, write a paper contrasting Islam and Christianity.

   • When contrasting two subjects you will be stressing the differences using transitional words such as *but, however, on the other hand, on the contrary, counter to, as opposed,* etc.

   • Your paper should touch on topics such as the question of sin. What about eternity? How does each religion teach how we are to live?

   • Your paper should also contrast Jesus and Mohammed since they are central to these two religions. For instance, what claims did each make? Did each perform miracles?

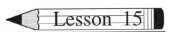

Chapters 18-22

1. a. If you need to, finish the paper you began in Lesson 14 contrasting Islam and Christianity.

   b. Read Chapter 18 "A Daring Plan." Narrate back to your teacher what you remember. Include as much detail as possible.

2. a. Before reading the last four chapters, discuss with your teacher what you think will happen to Hamid, Kinza, and Jenny. This is called **predicting an outcome**. How would you end the story?

   b. Read Chapters 19-22.

3. a. Who was the main character in the first part of the book?

   b. Who was the main character in the second part of the book?

   c. Each of these characters changed as the story was told. Write a paper for each character describing the ways in which they changed.

      1) How did Hamid change?

3.
a. Hamid
b. Jenny
c. Possible answers:
1) At the beginning of the story, Hamid was a little boy without hope. He did not have much faith in his mother's god or in the saints that were worshipped by his people. His main goal in life was to stay out of his cruel stepfather's way and to take care of his sister Kinza.
After getting Kinza settled with the English nurse, he found acceptance with a group of homeless city boys. When they visited the home of the nurse he heard about Jesus. He then came face to face with his sin and the price Jesus paid for that sin. As he heard more about Jesus' love and sacrifice, he began to change. This is evidenced by his kind treatment of a small starving kitten which he would normally not have even noticed.

When Kinza's safety is again threatened, Hamid confides in the nurse. She helps him rescue Kinza and Hamid sees his mother once more. She asks him to come home. He is afraid of his stepfather, but even more he wants to learn all he can about Jesus. So Hamid stays with the nurse, learning to read. As his love for Christ grows, he purposes to return to his family taking a Bible with him to share the good news, no longer afraid.

3.

c. Possible answer:

2) Jenny was a much loved, rather spoiled little girl. When we meet her she is recovering from an illness and her parents have been advised to take her to a warmer climate. They are going to visit her Aunt Rosemary who is a missionary nurse in Northern Africa. Jenny is excited about visiting this exotic location. Because of her love for children and a sincere desire to help, Jenny is drawn into her aunt's work. She decides she might like to be a missionary like her aunt. She is bewildered as her aunt explains to her that she cannot be a missionary and tell people about Jesus, because she doesn't know Him herself. Then Jenny begins her search for God.

2) How did Jenny change?

4.   Today, you will begin writing a book review of *Star of Light*. A **book review** is a kind of **persuasive writing** in which you give your opinion of the book, supporting that **opinion** with **facts** and details from the book. A book review may be written as a short one paragraph review or more in depth with several paragraphs.

You may choose one or more of the following as the subject for your paper:

1) **Plot -** the action that takes place in a story
Was it predictable?
Hard to believe?
Was the climax interesting?
What were some major events?
Were you surprised at the ending?

2) **Characters -** the people in the story
How did they change in the story?
What were their major personality traits?
Could you identify with them?

3) **Setting -** where the story takes place
Was the setting important to the story?
Why or why not?
Did you learn more about this part of the world?
Was it believable?

4) **Theme -** what the author wants to teach through the story
These could include greed, courage, love, self-sacrifice, faith, etc.

5. a. Complete your book review today.

   b. Optional: You may wish to make your review into a booklet and decorate the cover.

Assessment 4
(Lessons 13 - 15)

1. Read a chapter in a book and narrate what you read to your teacher.

2. Write a sentence illustrating the following: first person, second person and third person.

3. What is an analogy?

1. Self - explanatory
   Narration is the retelling of the story in your own words.
2. Possible answers:
   I like ice cream.
   (first person)
   You like ice cream.
   (second person)
   He likes ice cream.
   (third person)
3. An analogy is the comparison of unfamiliar ideas with something that is simple or more familiar.

Mary Drewery (1918 -) brings the Reformation period to life in *Devil in Print*. In order to insure the accuracy of the book, she covered every step of Tom's journey into exile and home again. Mrs. Drewery's long time involvement with the Scout movement in England has enhanced her understanding of children and the stories they like.

✎ **Teacher's Note: As your student completes this lesson, choose skills from the *Review Activities* that he needs. The *Review Activities* follow this lesson.**

1.
c. -ing   -ingly
  1) amazing   amazingly
  2) surprising surprisingly
  3) longing   longingly
  4) according   accordingly

      Adj   N   V   Adj
d. The boys descended the
        Adj   N
  shadowy stairs.

The boys tiptoed down the shadowy stairs. Each creak of the uneven treads seemed agonizingly loud and as though it must surely waken the sleepers in the room above. A thin line of light showed under the door of the printing shop. Tom drummed lightly on the panel with his fingertips.

Devil in Print by Mary Drewery

1. a. Take the literature passage from dictation. Proofread, looking for any spelling or punctuation errors.

    b. Make a spelling list to study this week or use the following suggested list: treads, agonizingly, panel, shadowy.

        Before you add a suffix beginning with a vowel, look at the root word. If the root word ends with a silent **e**, drop the **e** before adding the suffix.

        > **Spelling Tip**
        > Words ending with a silent **e**, must drop the **e** before adding a suffix beginning with a vowel.

    c. Add the suffix.
        -ing   **-ingly**
        Ex: agonize   agonizing   agonizingly
        1) amaze
        2) surprise
        3) long
        4) accord

    d. Label the parts of speech in the following sentence. Label articles as adjectives.
        N(Noun), **V**(Verb), **Adj**(Adjective):

        The boys descended the shadowy stairs.

2. a. Read the following sentence:

> *The ball fell down.*

1) What is the subject?
2) What is the verb?
3) Where did the ball fall?

b. *Down* tells where the ball fell. *Down* is an adverb. **Adverbs** modify verbs, adjectives, and other adverbs. Like adjectives, adverbs help to bring these words into "focus" or clarify the meaning of verbs, adjectives, and other adverbs.

Adverbs answer three main groups of questions:
- Time - when? how often?
- Place - where?
- Manner - how? how much? to what extent?

c. Look at the last sentence of the literature passage.
1) What is the subject?
2) What is the verb?
3) What word describes how Tom drummed?

d. Adjectives usually appear before the noun they modify, but adverbs usually do <u>not</u> appear before the verbs they modify. Adverbs often appear after the verb or after the direct object (if there is one), but many appear between a helping verb and the main verb. Sometimes they even appear before the complete predicate or before the complete subject, at the beginning of a sentence.

Ex: Tom drummed *lightly* on the panel with his fingertips.
Tom *lightly* drummed on the panel with his fingertips.
Lightly, Tom drummed on the panel with his fingertips.
Tom drummed on the panel *lightly* with his fingertips.
Tom drummed on the panel with his fingertips *lightly*.

Although some of these sound a little awkward, they still make sense.

2.
a. 1) ball
2) fell
3) down

c. 1) Tom
2) drummed
3) lightly(adverb)

2.
e. agonizingly loud

f. Possible answers:
1) *Today*, each creak was loud.
2) The light showed *faintly* under the door.
3) Tom drummed *frequently* on the panel.
4) The noise awakened the sleepers *downstairs*.

✏ **Teacher's Note:**
Printing shop may be considered a noun, or *printing* may be considered an adjective, describing what kind of *shop*.

g. shadowy stairs

each creak

uneven treads

thin line

✏ **Teacher's Note:**
Disregard the word *loud*. This is a predicate adjective.

3.
a.1) Tom took the book reverently. (how)
2) Tom was yawning sleepily. (how)
3) Cochlaeuss' shrewd mind was immediately alert. (when)
4) Tyndale listened gravely. (how)
5) Tom looked around wildly. (around-where) (wildly-how)

e. Look at the second sentence of the literature passage. Write the two words that tell how the creaking stairs seemed. The second word you wrote is an adjective. The first word you wrote is an adverb answering the question *how*. An adverb can describe a verb, adjective, or another adverb.

f. Add different adverbs to the following sentences:
Ex: The boys tiptoed.
     Today, the boys tiptoed. (tells when)
     The boys tiptoed *downstairs*. (tells where)
     The boys tiptoed *quietly*. (tells how)
     Sometimes, the boys tiptoed. (tells how often)

1) Each creak was loud.
   Add an adverb telling <u>when</u> it creaked.
2) The light showed under the door.
   Add an adverb telling <u>how</u> the light showed.
3) Tom drummed on the panel.
   Add an adverb telling <u>how often</u> Tom drummed.
4) The noise awakened the sleepers.
   Add an adverb telling <u>where</u> the noise awakened.

g. Do not confuse adjectives with adverbs. Remember, adjectives describe a person, place, thing, or idea. Underline all the adjectives in the literature passage. Draw an arrow from the adjective to the word it describes. (For this exercise, disregard articles, pronouns, and possessives.)

3. a. Look at the following sentences about *Devil in Print*. Underline the adverbs and tell what question they answer: how, when, where, to what extent.
   1) Tom took the book reverently.
   2) Tom was yawning sleepily.
   3) Cochlaeuss' shrewd mind was immediately alert.
   4) Tyndale listened gravely.
   5) Tom looked around wildly.

b. Now rewrite the sentences in **3a**, moving the adverb around as was done in **3d**. Notice that moving adverbs around can change the emphasis of the sentence.

c. List all the adverbs from the literature passage.

d. Of the five adverbs you underlined, what is the most common ending?

e. ADVERB ALERT!
Words ending in **-ly** is often a clue that the word is an adverb, but be careful. Not all words ending in **-ly** are adverbs; some are adjectives.
Ex: lovely day (*lovely* is an adjective describing the noun, *day*)
friendly neighbor (*friendly* is an adjective describing the noun, *neighbor*)

f. The word *not* or the contraction *n't* is an adverb although it does not answer the questions adverbs answer. It is used to make a sentence negative.

g. Adverbs are diagrammed on an angled line attached to the base line below the word modified.

adverb modifying a verb: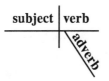

adverb modifying an adjective: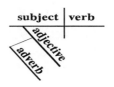

adverb modifying another adverb:

3.
b. 1) Reverently, Tom took the book.
Tom reverently took the book.
Tom took reverently the book.
Tom took the book reverently.

2) Sleepily, Tom was yawning.
Tom sleepily was yawning.
Tom was sleepily yawning.
Tom was yawning sleepily.

3) Immediately, Cochleuss' shrewd mind was alert.
Cochleuss' immediately shrewd mind was alert.
Cochleuss' shrewd mind immediately was alert.
Cochleuss' shrewd mind was alert immediately.

4) Gravely, Tyndale listened.
Tyndale gravely listened.
Tyndale listened gravely.

5) Wildly, Tom looked around.
Tom wildly looked around.
Tom looked wildly around.
Tom looked around wildly.

c. down, agonizingly, surely, above, lightly

d. Many adverbs end in -ly.

h.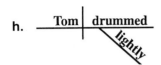

3.
i. 1) Scripture | was read — The / boldly

2) crowd | yelled — The / angrily

3) Jesus | answered — quietly

4) He | walked — away

5) They | did understand — n't

k. 1) **Texas' state flower**
   2) **boss's office or boss' office**

4.
Adj Adj   N   V
c. 1) **A small bird pecked**
        Adv
     nervously.
   Adj   N   V
   2) **Large waves crashed**
           Adv
      loudly.
   Adj   N   V
   3) **Bright daisies danced**
            Adv
      merrily.
        N   V   Adv
   4) **Bill played wildly.**

h. Diagram this sentence.

   Tom drummed lightly.

i. Diagram the following sentences.
   1) The Scripture was read boldly.
   2) The crowd yelled angrily.
   3) Jesus quietly answered.
   4) He walked away.
   5) They didn't understand.

j. Look at the sentences from **3a**. Look at the first word in the third sentence. *Cochlaeuss'* is a possessive noun. When you change a name ending in **s** into its possessive form, usually just add an apostrophe (')). If the name is a short one-syllable word, you usually add an apostrophe and **s** (**'s**). You may also just add an apostrophe.
   Ex: Mose**s'** staff or Le**s's** coat

k. Change the following nouns into its possessive form:
   1) the state flower of Texas
   2) the office belonging to the boss

l. Review your spelling words.

4. a. Practice identifying adverbs by using your easy-readers. Tell what question they answer.
                    OR
   b. Write five sentences with adverbs.
                    OR
   c. Using the following sentences, label the parts of speech. **N** (Noun), **V** (Verb), **Adj** (Adjective), **Adv** (Adverb), **Pro** (Pronoun)

   1) A small bird pecked nervously.
   2) Large waves crashed loudly.
   3) Bright daisies danced merrily.
   4) Bill played wildly.

d. Using the sentences in **4c**, diagram the subject, verb, adjective, and adverb. Every word will be diagrammed.

e. Optional: Take an oral or written spelling pretest.

5. a. Take the literature passage from dictation.
                        OR
    b. Look through your easy-readers again. Find five sentences that contain a subject, verb, adjective, and/or adverb. Diagram the sentences.
                        OR
    c. Choose skills from the *Review Activities* on the next page.

4.

d. 1)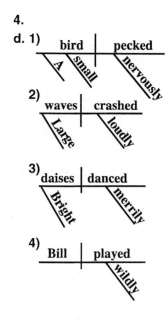

1.

a. <u>Leanne</u> | <u>walked</u> (away) (immediately)

b. <u>Ralph</u> | <u>has done</u> (well)

c. (Suddenly) the <u>phone</u> | <u>rang</u>.

d. The <u>stars</u> | <u>shone</u> (brightly).

e. <u>I</u> | <u>didn't go</u> (yesterday).

2.

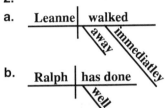

a. Leanne | walked / away / immediatley

b. Ralph | has done / well

c. phone | rang / the / Suddenly

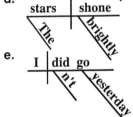

d. stars | shone / The / brightly

e. I | did go / n't / yesterday

3. Possible answers:

a. The *joggers'* path was lined with screaming fans.

b. Everyone applauded the *president's* speech.

c. The *audience's* reponse was astounding.

d. The dog was returned to the *children's* parents.

e. *Phineas'* heart was pounding as he waited anxiously in line.

Review Activities

Choose the skills your student needs to review.

1. *Subject/ Predicate; Verb, Adjective, Adverb*
Separate the complete subject and predicate with a vertical line. Underline the subject once and underline the verb twice. Circle the adverbs. Box the adjectives.

   a. Leanne walked away immediately.
   b. Ralph has done well.
   c. Suddenly, the phone rang.
   d. The stars shone brightly.
   e. I didn't go yesterday.

2. *Diagram*
Using the sentences above, diagram the subject, verb, adjective, and adverb. Every word will be diagrammed.

3. *Possessive Nouns*
Write the following words in its possessive form in a sentence.
   a. joggers
   b. president
   c. audience
   d. children
   e. Phineas

It was dusk of the sixth day since they had left Cologne. The morning and afternoon had had all the warmth of St. Martin's summer but now, as the sun sank below the horizon, white mist gathered over the water. One of the mid-stream mills built on pontoons loomed out of the wreathing vapor and the master put over his helm and steered for the shore. A voice hailed him from the bank. The tow-lines shortened and at last one of the crew was able to tie up the vessel to the wharf-side. The evening was still and quiet and peaceful, even here on the quay.

Devil in Print by Mary Drewery

Teacher's Note: As your student completes this lesson, choose skills from the *Review Activties* that he needs. The *Review Activities* follow this lesson.

1. a. Take the literature passage from dictation. Proofread, looking for any spelling or punctuation errors.

   b. Make a spelling list to study this week or use the following suggested list: Cologne, horizon, crew, vessel.

   By now you probably know **gn** and **kn** make a **/n/** sound. Words may begin with **gn** (as in *gnaw)* and **kn** (as in *knot*). Words may end in **gn**, but usually will not end in **kn**.

> ### Spelling Tip
> Gn and kn may begin a word;
> gn may end a word, but usually
> kn will not end a word.

Write the following words and underline the **kn** and **gn**. Say the words aloud as you write them.

gn at the beginning of a word	**kn** at the beginning of a word	**gn** at the end of a word
gnaw	know	reign
gnarl	knock	sovereign
gnash	knot	sign
gnome	knuckle	align

1.

Adj Adj   N   Conj Adj
d. The late morning and early
      N   V   Adv   Adj.
   afternoon was very warm.

✎ **Teacher's Note:**
Pronunciation may vary
depending on regional
accents.

c. Look up any unfamiliar words. (i.e. pontoons, quay) When using your dictionary, remember to use the guide words on the top of the page to help you find the words.

d. Label the parts of speech in the following sentence: **N** (Noun), **V** (Verb), **Adj** (Adjective), **Adv** (Adverb), **Conj** (Conjunction)

The late morning and early afternoon was very warm.

2. a. When you spell a word ending with a **/oo/** sound, it may be spelled with **ue** (as in *blue*) or it may be spelled with **ew** (as in *crew*). There are only a few words that end in **oo**.

> ### Spelling Tip
> Words ending in a **/oo/** sound may be spelled with **ue** or **ew**.

Write the following words. Say the words aloud as you write them. Underline **ew**, **ue**, and **oo**.

ew	ue	oo
blew	blue	too
dew	due	moo
crew	clue	coo
flew	glue	zoo
stew	issue	woo

2.
b.1) A <u>tall,</u> <u>broad</u> **man**
   stepped forward.
 2) My <u>new</u> **master was an**
   <u>unmarried</u> **man.**
 3) We stopped at the
   <u>principal</u> **hotel.**

b. Underline the adjectives in the following sentences. Do not include pronouns or articles.

1) A tall, broad man stepped forward.
2) My new master was an unmarried man.
3) We stopped at the principal hotel.

c. Look at the first sentence of the literature passage. What word describes *day*?

                                                             c. sixth

d. The last sentence in the literature passage uses three words to describe the evening. What are they?

                                                    d. still, quiet, peaceful

Since these adjectives are in the predicate part of the sentence and follow the verb, they are called predicate adjectives. A verb which links a word in the predicate to the subject is called a **linking verb. Predicate adjectives** follow a linking verb and describe the subject.

e. Sometimes the word following a linking verb doesn't describe the subject, it just renames the subject. A noun or pronoun following a linking verb that renames the subject is called a **predicate nominative**.

Read the following sentence:

    My father was the only boy in his family.

The verb *was* links the subject, *father,* to the noun *boy. Boy* is a predicate nominative because it renames (or identifies) *father*.

f. Look at the first sentence of the literature passage. "Since they had left Cologne" is a phrase that adds information, but cannot stand alone apart from the main part of the sentence, "It was dusk of the sixth day." This type of phrase is called a **dependent clause**. Look at the main part of the sentence. What is the subject of the sentence?

                                                    f. It

g. What is the verb?

                                                    g. was

h. What part of the sentence is *dusk*?

                                                h. a predicate nominative

3.

a.1) The old merchant
    was a generous <u>soul</u>.
  PN - renames *merch.*

2) He was a <u>fool</u>.
  PN - renames *fool*

3) Hans was a clumsy <u>oaf</u>.
  PN - renames *Hans*

4) The shop was <u>dim</u>.
  PA - describes *shop*

5) He is <u>sympathetic</u>.
  PA - describes *He*

3.

c. 1)

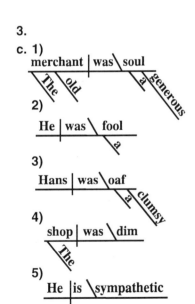

e.1) two hundred seventy-
    seven
 2) sixty-four
 3) eighty-five thousand
 4) seven hundred

3. a. After reviewing **2b-e** (and Lesson 10 if necessary), underline and label the predicate adjectives (**PA**) and predicate nominatives (**PN**) in the following sentences.

    Draw an arrow from the noun or adjective in the predicate to the word in the subject which it describes or renames.

    1) The old merchant was a generous soul.
    2) He was a fool.
    3) Hans was a clumsy oaf.
    4) The shop was dim.
    5) He is sympathetic.

 b. Both predicate adjectives and predicate nominatives are diagrammed the same way. Add a slanted line to the base line between the verb and either the predicate adjective or the predicate nominative. Any words modifying the predicate adjective or predicate nominative are placed on a slanted line below.

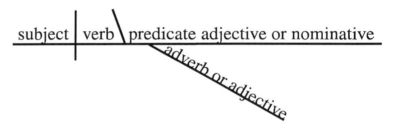

 c. Using the sentences in **3a**, diagram the subject, verb, adjective, predicate nominative, and predicate adjective.

 d. You learned that number words are adjectives. Today, you will learn how to use the **hyphen** (-) in number words. Number words from *twenty-one* to *ninety-nine* are spelled with hyphens. Number words like *five hundred* are not spelled with hyphens.
    Ex: twenty-one
        three hundred forty
        five thousand sixty-four
        seventy-nine

 e. Place hyphens correctly in the following number words.
    1) two hundred seventy seven
    2) sixty four
    3) eighty five thousand
    4) seven hundred

f. Review your spelling words.

4. a. Label each word in the following sentences. **N** (Noun),
        V (Verb), **Adj** (Adjectives), **PN** (Predicate Nominative),
        and **PA** (Predicate Adjective).
    1) The kind woman was delightful.
    2) The Raiders were the winners.
    3) Chris is a fisherman.
    4) Martha was a worker.
    5) Mary was a listener.
    6) Martha is angry.
    7) Mary is happier.

   b. Review **3b** on how to diagram predicate nominatives and
       predicate adjectives. Using the sentences in **4a**, diagram each
       word in every sentence.

   c. Look at the second sentence in the literature passage. Why is
       St. Martin's spelled with an apostrophe and **s** ('**s**)?

   d. Look at the fourth sentence in the literature passage. *A voice
       hailed him from the bank.* Think of some synonyms you
       could use to replace the underlined word. If you can't think
       of any words, try looking in a thesaurus. Which way sounds
       better to you?

   e. Optional: Take an oral or written spelling pretest.

5. a. Take the paragraph from dictation.
                          OR
   b. Practice identifying predicate adjectives and predicate
       nominatives by looking in your easy-readers.
                          OR
   c. Choose skills from the *Review Activities* on the next page.

4.
Adj Adj N V
a. 1) **The kind woman was**
   PA
   delightful.
   Adj N V Adj
   2) **The Raiders were the**
   PN
   winners.
   N V Adj. PN
   3) **Chris is a fisherman.**
   N V Adj. PN
   4) **Martha was a worker.**
   N N Adj. PN
   5) **Mary was a listener.**
   N V PA
   6) **Martha is angry.**
   N V PA
   7) **Mary is happier.**

4.
b. 1) woman | was \ delightful / The
   2) Raiders | were \ winners / The \ the
   3) Chris | is \ fisherman \ a
   4) Martha | was \ worker \ a
   5) Mary | was \ listener \ a
   6) Martha | is \ angry
   7) Mary | is \ happier

c. **It is telling of the summer
   of St. Martin. (possessive
   noun)**

d. **Possible answers:
   beckoned, called**

   Answers will vary.

115

1.

a.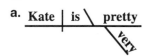

b.

c.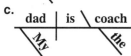

d.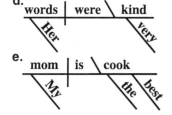

e.

2. Answers will vary.

3. Answers will vary.

4.
a. two hundred
b. seventy-four
c. one hundred fifty-five

Review Activities

Choose the skills your student needs to review.

1. *Diagram (Subject, Verb, Adjective, Adverb, Predicate Adjective, Predicate Nominative).*
   Diagram every word in the following sentences.
   a. Kate is very pretty.
   b. The dog was frisky.
   c. My dad is the coach.
   d. Her words were very kind.
   e. My mom is the best cook.

2. *Linking Verb / Predicate Adjective*
   Write a sentence using a linking verb and a predicate adjective. Draw an arrow from the predicate adjective to the word in the subject it describes.

3. *Linking Verb / Predicate Nominative*
   Write a sentence using a linking verb and a predicate nominative. Draw an arrow from the predicate nominative to the word in the subject it renames.

4. *Hyphens / Number Words*
   Correctly place the hyphens in the following number words.
   a. two hundred
   b. seventy four
   c. one hundred fifty five

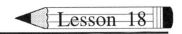

"How do you feel now, Tom?" came Tyndale's kindly voice. "You had us worried for a time when we saw you go down under that ruffian. Then there was so much to do to bring the ship under control that it was some time before we could attend to you."

"Anyway, your Bibles are safe, Sir William," said Tom.

"Yes, they are safe, Tom," replied Tyndale quietly. "Did you doubt for one moment but that God would protect His own?"

Devil in Print by Mary Drewery

1. a. Take this conversation from dictation. Written conversation is called **dialogue**. Proofread, looking for any spelling or punctuation errors.

    b. Make a spelling list to study this week or use the following suggested list: worried, doubt, protect, ruffian.

    Before adding a suffix beginning with a vowel (except **-ing**) to a word ending in **y**, look at the word. If the word ends with a consonant and **y**, change the **y** to **i**; if the word ends with a vowel and **y**, just add the suffix. The same rule applies when adding **s**.

> ### Spelling Tip
> Words ending in **y** preceded by a consonant must change the **y** to **i** before adding a suffix beginning with a vowel, except **-ing**; otherwise, just add the suffix.

Teacher's Note: As your student completes this lesson, choose skills from the *Review Activities* that he needs. The *Review Activities* follow this lesson.

1.

c.   s   -ed   -ing

1) hurries   hurried   hurrying
2) tries   tried   trying
3) cries   cried   crying
4) marries   married   marrying
5) plays   played   playing
6) stays   stayed   staying

e. Refer to the literature passage.

f. 1) "I'll see you tomorrow," said Steve.

   2) Anita asked, "Where are we meeting?"

   3) "We're meeting at noon," said Steve, "and going to the park."

c. Add **-s, -ed**, and **-ing** to the following words:

	s	-ed	-ing
Ex: worry	worries	worried	worrying
Ex: relay	relays	relayed	relaying
1) hurry			
2) try			
3) cry			
4) marry			
5) play			
6) stay			

d. How did you do with the quotation marks in your dictation? Read the following Quotation Rules.

Quotation Rules

1. Capitalize the first word in the quotation.
2. In a split quotation, do not capitalize the first word in the second part of the quotation.
3. The comma, exclamation mark, or question mark is placed inside the closing quotation mark.
4. Begin a new paragraph every time a new person speaks.
5. Put quotation marks around the actual words spoken or thought.

---

e. Look at the literature passage. Using one color pencil, underline the actual words spoken by Tyndale. Using another color pencil, underline the actual words spoken by Tom. This helps you see what words should be enclosed with quotation marks.

f. Add correct punctuation and capitalization.
1) I'll see you tomorrow said Steve
2) Anita asked where are we meeting
3) We're meeting at noon said Steve and going to the park

g. Look at the first sentence of the literature passage. Tyndale is speaking to Tom. The word *Tom* is set apart with a **comma** because he is the person addressed.

   Ex: Tom, put the book in your bag.
       Put the book in your bag, Tom.
       Put the book, Tom, in your bag.

   Write three sentences addressing a person, following the examples above.

2. a. Look at the first sentence of the last paragraph in the literature passage. The word *yes* is separated by a comma to show a mild interjection. If you need to review interjections, refer to Lesson 10. Label the parts of speech in the following sentences. **N** (Noun), **V** (Verb), **Pro** (Pronoun), **Adj** (Adjective), **Adv** (Adverb), **Int** (Interjection)

   1) Oh! It is not the same thing.
   2) Aye, it was.
   3) Oh yes, he does.
   4) Well, you've worked hard.

   b. Since interjections do not have a real part in a sentence, we do not diagram them with the sentence. They are added on a separate line just above the left end of the diagram.

   Interjection
   _____
   subject | verb
          |

   Ex: **Wow, you did** a good job.

   Wow
   _____
   You | did
        |

   c. Diagram the following sentences. The last one is a challenge. It contains a predicate nominative.

   1) Well, you've worked hard.
   2) Aye, it was.
   3) Oh yes, he does.
   4) Oh! It is not the same thing.

2.

     Int Pro V Adv Adj   Adj

a. 1) Oh! It is not the same
     N
   thing.
    Int Pro V

  2) Aye, it was.
      Int Pro V

  3) Oh yes, he does.
     Int   Pro V   V

  4) Well, you've worked
      Adv
   hard.

c. 1)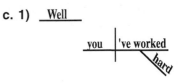

2)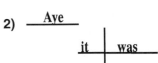

3)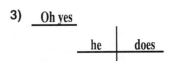

4)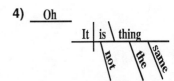

2.
d. predicate adjective

d. Look at the literature passage. In Tom's reply to Sir William, is the word *safe* a predicate adjective or a predicate nominative?

3. a. There are four types of sentences: one that makes a statement, one that asks a question, one that expresses strong emotion, and one that makes a command.

Declarative - It makes a statement and ends with a period. (.)
Ex: Ralph went hiking in the mountains.
Interrogative - It asks a question and ends with a question mark. (**?**)
Ex: Where did he go?
Exclamatory - It expresses strong or sudden emotion and ends with an exclamation mark. (**!**)
Ex: The Appalachian Trails are beautiful!
Imperative - It makes a command and ends with a period (.) or exclamation mark. (**!**)
Ex: Tell me all about your trip. OR
       Tell me all about your trip!

Read the following sentence again:

Tell me all about your trip.

Can you find the subject and verb? Some sentences do not name a subject, but it is understood. The subject in the above imperative sentence is *you*. To diagram this kind of sentence, place the subject where it normally is placed, but enclose it with parentheses.

(You)	tell

3.
b. 1) Marvin
  2) You
  3) I
  4) You

b. Name the subject in the following sentences.
  1) Marvin is coming to help us with the Drama Club.
  2) Thanks for coming.
  3) I'm glad to help in any way.
  4) Get the script.

c. Diagram only the subject and verb in the following sentence.

Get the script.

| **Hint** |
| An imperative sentence often does not state the subject; it is understood to be *you.* |

d. Look through your easy-readers to find interjections.

OR

e. Write your own sentences with interjections.

OR

f. Circle the interjections in the sentences provided below.
    1) Alas, he has gone.
    2) Well, you must be tired.
    3) Hey, come back here!
    4) Oh, this is too difficult.

g. Review your spelling words.

4. a. Today do a brief research about William Tyndale. Use an encyclopedia or visit your library. Write a **paragraph** with a few sentences, and use the following questions as a guide.

    Who was he?
    When did he live?
    Where did he live?
    What did he do?

    1) Begin your paragraph with a topic sentence. A **topic sentence** will tell what the paragraph is about.
    2) All the other sentences must support (or tell about) the topic sentence. These are called **supporting sentences.**
    3) Remember to begin your paragraph by indenting the first sentence.

3.

c. (You) | get

3.

f. 1) (Alas), he has gone.
  2) (Well), you must be tired.
  3) (Hey), come back here!
  4) (Oh), this is too difficult.

121

4.

b.1) I hope you'll come, Brad.

2) Casey, please come here.

3) I filled the bowls with peanuts, cashews, and almonds.

4) I will have a snack, play basketball, and read a book.

5) I'm sorry, Leslie, for being late.

6) My, what a lovely day.

7) Wow, the fireworks are great!

5.

      Adv   Adj   Adj

c. 1) Joyfully, the children's

     N   V   Adj   N

choir sang the anthem.

    Adj N   V   V   DO

2) His son had come home

          Adv

unexpectedly.

    Adj   Adj   N   V Adj

3) That funny clown is the

    Adj   PN

best juggler.

    Adj Adj   N   V   IO Adj

4) The big collie gave me a

    Adj DO

wet kiss.

    Adj   N V Adv PA

5) The bus is often late.

b. Add commas.

   1) I hope you'll come Brad.

   2) Casey please come here.

   3) I filled the bowls with peanuts cashews and almonds.

   4) I will have a snack play basketball and read a book.

   5) I'm sorry Leslie for being late.

   6) My what a lovely day.

   7) Wow the fireworks are great!

c. Optional: Take an oral or written spelling pretest.

5. a. Take the literature passage from dictation.

                OR

   b. Using your easy-readers, find the adjectives, subject, verb (helping verbs), adverbs, direct objects, indirect objects, predicate adjectives, and predicate nominatives. Show your teacher or write two examples of each.

                OR

   c. Label the sentence parts in the following sentences.
N (Noun), **V** (Verb), **Adj** (Adjective) **Adv** (Adverb)
IO (Indirect Object), **DO** (Direct Object)
PA (Predicate Adjective), **PN** (Predicate Nominative).

   1) Joyfully, the children's choir sang the anthem.

   2) His son had come home unexpectedly.

   3) That funny clown is the best juggler.

   4) The big collie gave me a wet kiss.

   5) The bus is often late.

Review Activities

Choose the skills your student needs to review.

1. *Noun, Verb, Adjective, Adverb, Interjection*
   Label the parts of speech **N** (Noun), **V**(Verb), **Adj**
   (Adjective) **Adv** (Adverb), **Int** (Interjection).

   a. Wow! Five little puppies were born yesterday.
   b. One small puppy shivered.
   c. The boy played well.
   d. The young girl sang sweetly.
   e. Oh, a volcano erupted today!

2. *Diagram (Subject, Verb, Adjective, Adverb, Interjection)*
   Diagram the sentences above.

3. *Commas (unequally modified)*
   Look at sentence **1a** above. Write the rule for explaining why
   a comma is not placed between the words *five* and *little*.

4. *Diagram (Interjection, Subject, Verb, Adverb, Adjective,
   Predicate Nominative, Predicate Adjective)*
   Using the following sentences, diagram all the sentence parts.

   a. Well, he is my best friend.
   b. Shh, you must be tired.
   c. Hey, come here!
   d. Oh, this is too difficult.

1.

       Int   Adj Adj   N
a. **Wow! Five little puppies**
       V   V   Adv
    were born yesterday.
      Adj   Adj   N
b. **One small puppy**
       V
    shivered.
      Adj N   V   Adv
c. **The boy played well.**
      Adj   Adj   N   V
d. **The young girl sang**
       Adv
    sweetly.
      Int Adj   N   V
e. **Oh, a volcano erupted**
      Adv
    today!

2.
a.

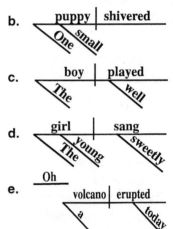

3. **A comma does not
   separate *five* and *little*
   because the words do
   not equally modify the
   word *puppies*.**

4.

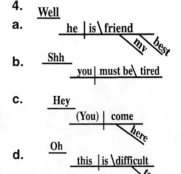

5.

a. Thank you, Mr. Morrison, for speaking to our class.
b. Mom, have you seen Sandy's glasses?
c. She may have left them at Lakeside Community Church.
d. "Tomorrow," Ron said, "we are having a party for Tim's aunt."
e. Oh, she found her glasses, Tom. or Oh! She found her glasses, Tom.

6.

a. beaches
b. companies
c. families
d. attorneys
e. sopranos
f. potatoes
g. stereos
h. loaves
i. hooves
j. knives

7.

a. Please sit down. (imperative)
b. Would you like a drink of water? (interrogative)
c. I am so thirsty! (exclamatory) or I am so thirsty. (declarative)
d. It was a hot day. (declarative)
e. Today was the hottest day of the year! (exclamatory)

5. *Punctuation and Capitalization*
Punctuate and capitalize correctly.

a. thank you mr morrison for speaking to our class
b. mom have you seen sandys glasses
c. she may have left them at lakeside community church
d. tomorrow ron said we are having a party for tims aunt
e. oh she found her glasses tom

6. *Plurals*
Write the following words in plural form.

a. beach
b. company
c. family
d. attorney
e. soprano
f. potato
g. stereo
h. loaf
i. hoof
j. knife

7. *Types of Sentences*
Punctuate the sentences. What kind of sentence is it?

a. Please sit down
b. Would you like a drink of water
c. I am so thirsty
d. It was a hot day
e. Today was the hottest day of the year

Assessment 5
(Lessons 16-18)

1. Underline the adverbs in the following sentences:

   a. The boys swam yesterday.
   b. The lamp tipped over.
   c. My cat naps often.
   d. Lindsey spoke quietly.
   e. Sometimes I run.

2. Diagram the sentences above.

3. What questions do adverbs answer?

4. What part of speech is *not*?

5. Indicate if the following sentences have a predicate adjective (**PA**) or predicate nominative (**PN**):

   a. John is my brother.
   b. He is funny.
   c. The pie tastes delicious.
   d. My dog is a cocker spaniel.

6. Diagram the sentences above.

7. Write a sentence with an interjection.

8. Diagram your sentence. Diagram only the interjection, subject, and verb.

1.
a. The boys swam <u>yesterday</u>.
b. The lamp tipped <u>over</u>.
c. My cat naps <u>often</u>.
d. Lindsey spoke <u>quietly</u>.
e. <u>Sometimes</u> I run.

2.
a.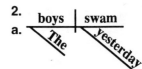

b.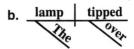

c.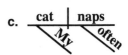

d.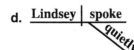

e.

3. When?, How?, How often?, How much? To what extent?

4. adverb

5. a. PN
   b. PA
   c. PA
   d. PN

6.
a. John | is \ brother
         \ my

b. He | is \ funny

c. pie | tastes \ delicious
   \ The

d. dog | is \ cocker spaniel
   \ My   \ a

7. Answers will vary.

8. Answers will vary.

The
Short Story Unit

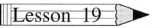

✏ Teacher's Note: The examples used in this lesson are not taken from short stories. They were chosen because the authors should be well-known to your student(s). The typical short story, although short, is much longer than what your student will write. Any good books your student(s) has read will help him become a better storyteller by providing good examples of the elements taught in this lesson.

✏ Teacher's Note: Two excellent books to help your young writer are:

1) *Written and Illustrated by...* by David Melton published by Landmark Editions
2) *Creating Books with Children* by Valerie Bendt published by Common Sense Press

1. People have always enjoyed stories. You know how exciting it sounds when someone says, "That reminds me of a story...." Starting from a very young age you were told and read stories. As you grew older you began to read stories on your own. Without knowing it you have gained much discernment about good storytelling. You have had experiences in your own life that would make a good story. The problem is writing it down in a clear and interesting way.

What makes a good story? David Melton, author of *Written and Illustrated by...,* says there are three basic elements of a story:

1) The beginning tells about the **setting** of the story, sets the **mood**, and introduces the **characters.**
2) The middle tells the **plot** and sets up a **conflict** or problem to be solved.
3) The end presents a **climax** and a solution to the problem or a resolution to the conflict.

Let's look at each one of these elements a little more closely.

Setting

First is the setting of the story. When you write a story you have to imagine where the characters are. The setting of the story tells when and where the story takes place:

I will begin the story of my adventures with a certain morning early in the month of June, the year of grace 1751, when I took the key for the last time out of the door of my father's house. The sun began to shine upon the summit of the hills as I went down the road; and by the time I had come as far as the manse, the blackbirds were whistling in the garden lilacs, and the mist that hung around the valley in the time of the dawn was beginning to arise and die away.

Kidnapped by Robert Louis Stevenson

The setting is important because very often it affects what the characters do.

Mood
The setting can also set the mood for the story, giving the reader a feeling of happiness, sadness, peacefulness, etc.:

This room was chill, because it seldom had a fire; it was silent, because remote from the nursery and kitchens; solemn, because it was known to be so seldom entered. The housemaid alone came here on Saturdays, to wipe from the mirrors and the furniture a week's quiet dust. And Mrs. Reed herself, at far intervals, visited it to review the contents of a certain secret drawer in the wardrobe, where were stored divers parchments, her jewel-casket, and a miniature of her deceased husband; and in those last words lies the secret of the bedroom - the spell which kept it so lonely in spite of its grandeur.

Jane Eyre by Charlotte Bronte

Using books on your shelf, look for passages describing different settings. Also, note if a mood is suggested.

2. **Characters**
The next important element of a short story that comes in the beginning of the story is the introduction of the characters. If you tell what a character looks like and describe his mannerisms, then your readers begin to feel they know him:

I remember him as if it were yesterday, as he came plodding to the inn door, his sea-chest following behind him in a hand-barrow - a tall, strong, heavy, nut-brown man, his tarry pigtail falling over the shoulders of his black, broken nails, and the sabre cut across one cheek, a dirty, livid white. I remember him looking round the cove and whistling to himself as he did so, and then breaking out in that old sea-song that he sang so often afterwards.

Treasure Island by Robert Louis Stevenson

Dialogue

A short story, unlike a novel, is short enough to be read comfortably in one sitting. Because it is short you cannot spend a lot of time describing the setting or the characters. The development of characters is best done through the action of the story. The dialogue (what the character says) will also give your readers further information about him or her:

"A merry Christmas, uncle! God save you!" cried a cheerful voice. It was the voice of Scrooge's nephew, who came upon him so quickly that this was the first intimation he had of his approach.

"Bah!" said Scrooge. "Humbug!" He had so heated himself with rapid walking in the fog and frost, this nephew of Scrooge's, that he was all in a glow; his face was ruddy and handsome; his eyes sparkled, and his breath smoked again.

"Christmas a humbug, uncle?" said Scrooge's nephew. "You don't mean that, I am sure!"

"I do," said Scrooge. "Merry Christmas! What right have you to be merry? What reason have you to be merry? You're poor enough."

"Come, then," returned the nephew gaily. "What right have you to be dismal? What reason have you to be morose? You're rich enough."

Scrooge, having no better answer ready on the spur of the moment, said, "Bah!" again; and followed it up with "Humbug!"

A Christmas Carol by Charles Dickens

Without using dialogue, you are just narrating a story. You can tell the story quicker, but it will not be as interesting. Conversation makes you feel as if you are listening to the characters and are part of the story. Both the setting and description of the characters can be revealed through the dialogue:

After welcoming their sisters, they triumphantly displayed a table set out with such cold meat as an inn larder usually affords, exclaiming, "Is not this nice? Is not this an agreeable surprise?"

"And we mean to treat you all," added Lydia; "but you must lend us the money, for we have just spent ours at the shop out there." Then, showing her purchases, "Look here, I have bought this bonnet. I do not think it is very pretty; but I thought I might as well buy it as not. I shall pull it to pieces as soon as I get home, and see if I can make it up any better." And when the sisters abused it as ugly, she added, with perfect unconcern, "Oh! but there were two or three much uglier in the shop; and when I have bought some prettier-coloured satin to trim it with fresh, I think it will be very tolerable."

Pride and Prejudice by Jane Austen

Using books on your shelves, scan for descriptions of characters.

3. Plot

Finally, the plot of the story tells the action. There are four general steps to develop the plot of the story:

1) Introduction
2) Conflict
3) Climax
4) Resolution

1) Introduction

We have already discussed the introduction which defines the setting and the mood and introduces the main characters.

2) Conflict

A conflict is a problem the main character has to deal with. There is usually one major complication in a short story, but there may develop several smaller ones as the story progresses. These create tension and hold the reader's interest. The conflict faced may be an internal conflict (such as conquering shyness) or an external conflict (such as solving a mystery).

3) **Climax**
   The climax is the turning point of the story and should be the most exciting part.

4) **Resolution**
   The resolution finishes the story, tying up all the loose ends.

Think about the following familiar fairy tales.

"Little Red Riding Hood"
"The Three Little Pigs"
"The Three Bears"
"The Princess and the Pea"

- What is the conflict in each one?
- When does the climax take place?
- How is the conflict resolved?

"Little Red Riding Hood":
Conflict: Little Red Riding Hood needs to take a basket to her grandma. Unknown to her, there is a hungry wolf in the woods.
Climax: Little Red Riding Hood discovers the wolf in her grandma's bed.
Resolution: Woodsman kills wolf or chases him away.

"The Three Little Pigs":
Conflict: Pigs need safe housing to keep them away from the hungry wolf.
Climax: Wolf tries to come down third little pig's chimney.
Resolution: Wolf falls into hot water and is no longer a threat.

"The Three Bears":
Conflict: Goldilocks is lost in the woods.
Climax: Goldilocks is found in the little bear's bed.
Resolution: Goldilocks runs home.

"The Princess and the Pea":
Conflict: Prince has to marry only a true Princess.
Climax: Princess complains of her bruises.
Resolution: Prince and Princess marry.

Discuss with your teacher some of your favorite stories, identifying the conflict, climax, and resolution in each.

4 & 5. Spend the next two days thinking about your story. Where do you get a good idea for a story? The best place is your own experience. Perhaps you can think of a problem or conflict you experienced in the past. This could become the basis for your short story.

Often, people tell other people's stories. The *Grandma's Attic* series and *Caddie Woodlawn* are the retelling of someone else's experiences. Ask your parents, grandparents, aunts, uncles, friends, etc. to tell you about something that happened to them while they were growing up. Then retell their story or use the story as a basis for another story. **Historical fiction** is an example of using a factual event and building a story around it.

Another idea is to rewrite a familiar story, like a fairy tale, giving it a different twist. I once read a funny retelling of the three little pigs from the wolf's point of view. If you would like to get it from your library, it is called *The True Story of the Three Little Pigs* by Jon Scieszka.

Finally, your story idea may just come out of your imagination. It could be set in the future or in a land that you make up. Listed here are some prewriting tips.

Prewriting Tips

1) Before you begin writing, spend some time today and tomorrow reviewing books and stories you have read in the past.
2) Look for the basic elements of setting, character, and plot.
3) Discuss the conflict and resolution of each story with your teacher.
4) Then, write down some brief possible story ideas.

This week, you will begin writing your story.

1) Look over the list of story ideas you made last week.

2) How should you begin writing your story? First remember to keep it simple.

3) Start with a few characters and one main problem.

4) A basic setting and short time span will also help. Some writers like to begin their stories right in the middle of the action, but you can also begin by describing the scene and characters and then move into the action.

5) Remember, it is best to let your characters "tell" the story by using dialogue, instead of using only narration.

6) Choose one story idea and begin writing. Looking at a blank sheet of paper may be the hardest part for you. David Melton calls this *"conquering the power of the white."* The best way to do this is to just begin writing. Get some ideas down. Your story doesn't have to flow or even be smoothly connected at this point. Just start writing!

7) Spend this week writing and developing your story. Some people find it very helpful to discuss their ideas as they go along. Talking it out seems to help make things more clear. Ask your teacher to help you with this.

Optional: You might find it enjoyable and profitable to begin a writers' club with several of your friends. Meeting together and reading your stories or even just parts of your stories aloud can be a great motivator and help to stimulate ideas.

1) This week, edit your story.

2) Use the Checklist below to assist you in your editing.

3) Make a final copy on a separate sheet of paper.

4) Optional: You might also enjoy illustrating your story.

5) *Creating Books With Children* by Valerie Bendt is an excellent resource that will tell you how to write and bind your story into book form.

You have put a lot of work into this project, so share it with others.

Checklist

1. Have you chosen an interesting title? ❏

2. Is your setting clear? ❏

3. Do your characters fit in the setting? ❏

4. Does your dialogue match your characters? ❏
   Is it believable?

5. Is your plot clear? ❏

6. Do the events of your story follow a ❏
   logical pattern?

7. Do you resolve the conflict? ❏

---

a. where and when the story takes place
b. a problem the main character has to deal with
c. the turning point of the story, usually the most exciting part
d. finishes the story

Student should give his own examples.

Assessment 6
(Lessons 19 - 21)

Define the elements of a short story listed below. Give an example for each element for stories you have read:

a. setting
b. conflict
c. climax
d. resolution

The waters of the bay were dancing in the sunshine. A fresh wind stirred the chestnut-trees with a pleasant sound, and the garden below was full of roses, butterflies, and bees. A great chirping and twittering went on among the birds, busy with their summer housekeeping, and, far away, the white-winged gulls were dipping and diving in the sea, where ships, like larger birds, went sailing to and fro.

Eight Cousins by Louisa May Alcott

1. a. Take the literature passage from dictation. Proofread, looking for any spelling or punctuation errors.

   b. Make a spelling list to study this week or use the following suggested list: dancing, pleasant, butterflies, housekeeping.

   Before adding a suffix, look at the word. If the root word ends with a silent **e**, drop the **e** before adding a suffix beginning with a vowel. If you are adding a suffix beginning with a consonant, just add the suffix.

   ### Spelling Tip
   In words which end with a silent **e**, drop the **e** before adding a suffix beginning with a vowel. Therefore, keep the **e** when adding a suffix beginning with a consonant.

   c. Complete the following chart.

	-ed	-ing	-ment
Ex: amaze	amazed	amazing	amazement
1) retire			
2) require			
3) confine			
4) bereave			
5) place			
6) commence			
7) improve			

Louisa May Alcott (1832 - 1888) is best known for her book, *Little Women,* which was largely based on her own life. Louisa's father was a noted educator and taught Louisa and her sisters at home. Because of her father's poor investments in idealistic projects, she spent most of her childhood in poverty. Louisa began at an early age to help support her family. When a publisher urged her to write a book for girls, she reluctantly agreed and in just six weeks she completed *Little Women.* Critics have noted that every chapter of the book is a complete story by itself, each presenting a conflict and resolution.

✎ Teacher's Note: As your student completes this lesson, choose skills from the *Review Activties* that he needs. The *Review Activities* follow this lesson.

1.
c. -ed   -ing
   1) retired   retiring
   2) required   requiring
   3) confined   confining
   4) bereaved   bereaving
   5) placed   placing
   6) commenced
                  commencing
   7) improved   improving

-ment
1) retirement
2) requirement
3) confinement
4) bereavement
5) placement
6) commencement
7) improvement

1.

    Adv   Adj   N
d. Yesterday, Mr. Wilson's tree
Conj Pro Adj   N   V
and our front gate fell
    Adv
down.

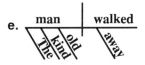

e.

2.
a. waters

b. were dancing

d. of, in, with, of, among,
   with, in, like

✎ **Teacher's Note: Some**
words look like
prepositions but are often
adverbs. A preposition
must have an object.

d. Label the parts of speech in the following sentence. **N** (Noun), **V** (Verb), **Adj** (Adjective), **Adv** (Adverb), **Pro** (Pronoun), **Conj** (Conjunction)

Yesterday, Mr. Wilson's tree and our front gate fell down.

e. Diagram every word in the following sentence.

The kind, old man walked away.

2. a. What is the subject of the first sentence in the literature passage?

   b. What is the verb?

   c. Between the subject and the verb is a phrase *of the bay*. The word *of* shows the connection between the words *waters* and *bay*. It is called a **preposition**. A preposition is a word that shows a connection or relationship between a noun or pronoun and another word in the sentence. You should become familiar with them.

Common Prepositions					
about	above	across	after	against	along
around	at	behind	below	beneath	beside
between	by	down	for	from	in
into	like	of	on	over	to
through	toward	under	up	upon	with
throughout	underneath				

   d. Using the literature passage, circle all the prepositions you can find.

   e. Underline the noun *bay* in the first sentence. The phrase *of the bay* begins with the preposition *of* and ends with the noun *bay*. This is a prepositional phrase. A **prepositional phrase** is made up of a preposition and a noun phrase (a noun or pronoun and any adjectives modifying it). The main noun or pronoun in the noun phrase is called the **object of the preposition**.

f. Underline all the objects of the prepositions you circled in this paragraph.

g. Is *on* in the third sentence of the literature passage a preposition?

h. Why or why not?

In order for a word to be a preposition it must have an **object**. If it does not, it is usually an adverb.
Ex: I fell *down*. (*Down* is an adverb describing where I fell.)
I fell *down* the stairs. (*Down* is a preposition because it has an object, *stairs*.)

i. The first sentence has two prepositional phrases. The first is *of the bay*. What is the second prepositional phrase?

j. If these phrases were removed from the sentence, would the sentence still make sense?

k. While prepositional phrases are not always necessary to the meaning of the sentence, they have a very important job. Prepositional phrases help to modify certain words in the sentence. Do you remember what other types of words modify?

l. Prepositional phrases perform the same job as adjectives and adverbs. These phrases can be an adjective phrase or an adverb phrase. The **adjective phrase** can be used to modify a noun or pronoun. It will answer the same questions that a single-word adjective could answer: What kind? Which one? How many or how much? Unlike the single-word adjective, though, the adjective phrase follows the noun or pronoun it modifies.
Ex: The boy *with the brown hair* stood up.
With the brown hair is a prepositional phrase describing which *boy*; therefore, it is an adjective phrase.

2.
f. of the <u>bay</u>; in the <u>sunshine</u>; with a pleasant <u>sound</u>; of roses, <u>butterflies</u>, and <u>bees</u>; among <u>birds</u>; with their summer <u>housekeeping</u>; in the <u>sea</u>; like larger <u>birds</u>

g. No

h. It doesn't have an object. It is an adverb.

i. in the sunshine

j. Yes, "the waters were dancing" would still make sense.

k. Adjectives modify nouns; adverbs modify verbs, adjectives, or other adverbs.

2.

n. The phrase "of the bay" decribes which waters.

o. "In the sunshine" decribes where the dancing was.

p. with a pleasant sound (adverb phrase)
of roses, butterflies, and bees (adjective phrase)
with their summer housekeeping (adverb phrase)
in the sea (adverb phrase)
like larger birds (adjective phrase)

3.
a. A fresh wind

b. stirred the chestnut-trees with a pleasant sound

c. The garden below

d. was full of roses, butterflies, and bees

e. A comma and the conjunction *and*

m. The **adverb phrase** modifies a verb, adjective, or adverb. It usually modifies the verb of the sentence. Like a single-word adverb, the adverb phrase answers the questions: Where? When? How? How often? How much? To what extent? Also, like a single-word adverb, the adverb phrase can often be moved from one part of the sentence to another.
Ex: The boy stood *on the stage.*

On the stage is a prepositional phrase describing where he *stood*; therefore, it is an adverb phrase.

n. Look at the prepositional phrases in the first sentence of the literature passage. Which one is an adjective phrase?

o. Which one is an adverb phrase?

p. Look at the prepositional phrases in the second sentence of the literature passage. Are they adjective phrases or adverb phrases?

q. Review your spelling words.

3. a. Look at the second sentence of the literature passage. The first part of the sentence says, *"A fresh wind stirred the chestnut-trees with a pleasant sound."* This is a complete sentence because it contains a subject and a predicate. What is the complete subject?

b. What is the predicate?

c. The second part of the sentence says, *"The garden below was full of roses, butterflies, and bees."* This is also a complete sentence, because it contains a subject and predicate. What is the complete subject?

d. What is the complete predicate?

e. What joins the two sentences?

Two or more sentences joined together with a conjunction is called a **compound sentence.**

List of Common Conjunctions			
and	but	or	so

f. Write the following sentences as compound sentences. Choose the best conjunction, and remember to place the comma before the conjunction.
Ex: We will read the story today. We will discuss it tomorrow.
We will read the story today, and we will discuss it tomorrow.

1) The storm tossed the ship. The men cried out in fear.
2) Jesus woke up. He calmed the storm.
3) Jamie likes blueberries. I like strawberries.
4) You may go to the library. You may stay home.
5) Our library books were overdue.   We had to pay a fine.

g. Read the following sentence.

Jesus and his disciples fed the multitudes.

What is the subject of the sentence?
When a sentence contains more than one subject doing one thing, it is called a **compound subject.**

h. Now, read this sentence.

Jesus prayed and wept.

What is the verb?
When a sentence contains a subject doing more than one thing it is called a **compound verb**.

i. Sometimes, a compound sentence may contain a compound subject, a compound verb, or both.
Read the following sentences.

Jesus and his disciples fed the multitudes, and the *men and women* were filled. (This a compound sentence with two compound subjects.)

Jesus *prayed and wept*, and the disciples slept. (This is a compound sentence with a compound verb.)

3.
f. 1) The storm tossed the ship, and the men cried out in fear.
2) Jesus woke up, and he calmed the storm.
3) Jamie likes blueberries, but I like strawberries.
4) You may go to the library, or you may stay home.
5) Our library books were overdue, so we had to pay a fine.

g. Jesus and his disciples

h. prayed and wept

3.

j. Answers will vary.

k. Answers will vary.

l. Answers will vary.

4.

a. A great chirping and twittering went on among the birds, busy with their summer housekeeping. Far away, the white-winged gulls were dipping and diving in the sea, where ships, like larger birds, went sailing to and fro.

b. subject-chirping and twittering; verb-went

c. subject-gulls; verb-were dipping and diving.

e.1) Swimming is my favorite hobby.
2) My brother enjoys hiking and bicycling.

j. Write a compound sentence.

k. Write a sentence containing a compound subject.

l. Write a sentence containing a compound verb.

4. a. Look at the last sentence of the literature passage. Try writing this compound sentence as two sentences. End your first sentence with the word *housekeeping*. Begin the second sentence with the word *Far*. Remember, a sentence must contain a subject and a verb.

    b. Looking at your new sentences, what is the subject and verb of your first sentence?

    c. What is the subject and verb of your second sentence?

    d. Perhaps you had a little difficulty finding the subject in the first sentence. At first glance, words like *chirping* and *twittering* look like verbs. Sometimes, verb forms ending in **-ing** are used as nouns. This is called a **gerund.**

    e. Underline the gerund.
        1) Swimming is my favorite hobby.
        2) My brother enjoys hiking and bicycling.

    f. Since prepositional phrases can modify the subject or the verb, they are diagrammed under the word they modify. This is how an adjective phrase is diagrammed:

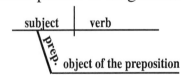

    g. This is how an adverb phrase modifying a verb is diagrammed:

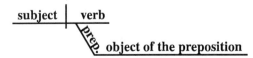

h. A prepositional phrase can also modify the direct object of a sentence. This is how it would be diagrammed:

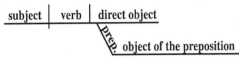

i. A prepositional phrase can also modify the predicate nominative or predicate adjective. This is how it would be diagrammed.

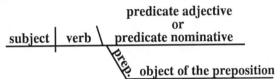

j. Diagram the following sentences (subject, adjective, adverbs, verbs, prepositional phrases, direct objects, predicate nominatives, predicate adjectives). Diagram every word in each sentence.
    1) The waters of the bay were dancing in the sunshine.
    2) A fresh wind stirred in the chestnut trees.
    3) The garden below was full of roses.
    4) A great chirping went on among the birds.
    5) The white-winged gulls were dipping in the sea.
    6) My father is the mayor.
    7) Sherry broke the lamp.

k. Optional: Take an oral or written spelling pretest.

5. a. Take the literature passage from dictation.
              OR
    b. Using any of your books, make a list of as many prepositions as you can find. Which ones are used the most?
              OR
    c. Write three sentences using prepositional phrases. A sentence may have more than one prepositional phrase. Put parentheses around the prepositional phrase, underline the preposition, and circle the object of the preposition.
              OR
    d. Choose skills from the *Review Activities* on the next page.

4

j.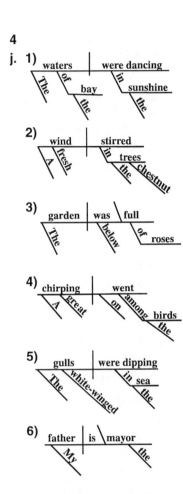

143

1.

a.
    V   Adj   N
Answer the phone.

b.
    V   prep   Adj
Sneaking around the
   N   Adj   N   V
corner, the officer captured
  Adj Adj   N
the stray dog.

c.
  Int   Adj N   V   V
Oh, the key is locked
   Prep   Adj   N
inside the car!

d.
  Adj   N   conj   N   V
The guitar and banjo are
  Prep N
on sale.

e.
   N   Adv   V
Marsha slowly opened
  Adj   Adj   N
her weary eyes.

2.

a. **The Dillsboro Chamber of Commerce was established in May 14, 1962.**

b. **"Ladies and gentlemen," said the announcer, "we are proud to introduce our speaker, Dr. James M. Mason."**

c. **We drove through Georgia, Alabama, and Tennessee.**

d. **It rained during our vacation, but we still had fun.**

e. **Paul flew to Australia and New Zealand.**

3.

a. prep
b. adv
c. adv
d. prep
e. adv

4. Answers will vary.

Review Activities

Choose the skills your student needs to review.

1. *Parts of Speech N (Noun), V (Verb), Adj (Adjective), Adv (Adverb), Pro (Pronoun), Prep (Preposition), Conj (Conjunction), Int (Interjection)*
   Label the parts of speech in the following sentences:

   a. Answer the phone.
   b. Sneaking around the corner, the officer captured the stray dog.
   c. Oh, the key is locked inside the car!
   d. The guitar and banjo are on sale.
   e. Marsha slowly opened her weary eyes.

2. *Capitalization and Punctuation*
   Capitalize and punctuate.

   a. the dillsboro chamber of commerce was established in may 14 1962
   b. ladies and gentlemen said the announcer we are proud to introduce our speaker dr james m mason
   c. we drove through georgia alabama and tennessee
   d. it rained during our vacation but we still had fun
   e. paul flew to australia and new zealand

3. *Preposition or Adverb*
   Read the following sentences. Is the underlined word a preposition (**Prep**) or an adverb (**Adv**)?

   a. The boy walked <u>through</u> the woods.
   b. The water seeped <u>through</u>.
   c. The cup tipped <u>over</u>.
   d. The deer pranced <u>over</u> the fence.
   e. I will swim <u>across</u>.

4. *Gerund*
   Write a sentence using a gerund.

5. *Diagram*

Diagram the subject, verb, adjective, prepositional phrase, direct object and predicate adjective in the sentences. Write if the prepositional phrase is an adjective (**Adj**) or an adverb (**Adv**) phrase. Every word will be diagrammed.

a. The doctor's office was filled with children.
b. The little boy with freckles was sunburnt.
c. Sara played with an orchestra.
d. I will eat around noon.
e. The apple on the tree fell to the ground.
f. She played a song on the piano.
g. The water gurgled under the bridge.
h. A pack of seeds scattered over the table.

6. Write a compound sentence.

7. Write a sentence containing a compound subject.

8. Write a sentence containing a compound verb.

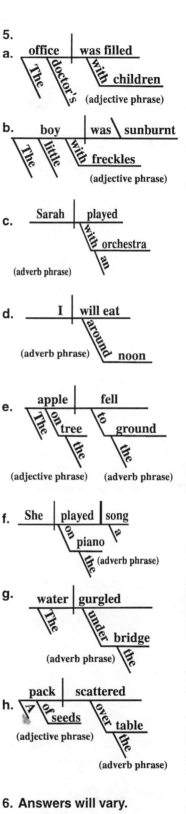

5.
a. (adjective phrase)
b. (adjective phrase)
c. (adverb phrase)
d. (adverb phrase)
e. (adjective phrase) (adverb phrase)
f. (adverb phrase)
g. (adverb phrase)
h. (adjective phrase) (adverb phrase)

6. Answers will vary.

7. Answers will vary.

8. Answers will vary.

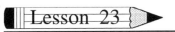
Teacher's Note: As your student completes this lesson, choose skills from the *Review Activties* that he needs. The *Review Activities* follow this lesson.

At his cry of rapture, the other lads looked up and smiled involuntarily, for the little kinswoman standing there above was a winsome sight with her shy, soft eyes, bright hair, and laughing face. The black frock reminded them of her loss, and filled the boyish hearts with a kindly desire to be good to "our cousin," who had no longer any home but this.

Eight Cousins *by Louisa May Alcott*

1. a. Take the literature passage from dictation. Proofread, looking for any spelling or punctuation errors.

   b. Make a spelling list to study this week or use the following suggested list: rapture, involuntarily, winsome, reminded.

   Often words with the **/cher/** sound at the end of a root word is spelled **-ture**.

   > ## Spelling Tip
   > Often, suffixes with a **/cher/** sound at the end of a root word will be spelled **-ture**.

   c. Write the following words and underline **-ture**. Say the words aloud as you write them.

nature	lecture	rapture
pasture	culture	tincture
miniature	gesture	adventure

   d. Why do you think quotation marks are used around *our cousin*?

   e. How did you do with the commas in your dictation? Look at the first sentence of the literature passage. Write a rule explaining why a comma separates the words *shy* and *soft*.

d. Quotation marks can be used to show that a word or phrase is used in a special way.

e. Separate two or more adjectives with commas.

f. Now, write your own sentence applying this rule.

g. Looking at the same sentence in the literature passage, write a rule explaining why a comma follows the words *eyes* and *hair*.

h. Write a sentence applying this rule.

2. a. Before adding **-ly** to words ending in **y** preceded by a consonant, change the **y** to **i** before adding **-ly**.

> ### Spelling Tip
> When adding the suffix **-ly** to words ending in a consonant and **y**, change the **y** to **i** before adding **-ly**.

Complete the chart.

                               -ly
Ex: voluntary   voluntarily
1) merry
2) momentary
3) necessary
4) ordinary
5) happy

b. Read the following simplified sentence taken from the literature passage.

The kinswoman had soft eyes, bright hair, and a laughing face.

Circle the word *and*. What two words (items) does it join? The word *and* is a conjunction.

List of Common Conjunctions
and   but   or   so

---

f. **Answers will vary.**

g. **Separate two or more phrases with a comma.**

h. **Answers will vary.**

2.
a. **1) merrily**
   2) momentarily
   3) necessarily
   4) ordinarily
   5) happily

b. **bright hair and a laughing face**

2.
c. 1) and
**   2) and**
**   3) or**

d. and, for, and, and, but

c. Circle the conjunctions in the following sentences.
   1) The aquarium held tetras, guppies, and neons.
   2) Setting up an aquarium requires equipment, knowledge, and patience.
   3) You may choose the apple, peach, or blueberry yogurt.

d. Circle all the conjunctions in the literature passage.

3. a. Conjunctions are also used to join two sentences. Punctuate a compound sentence with a comma <u>before</u> the conjunction. To tell if the sentence is a compound sentence, read the first part separately. Does it have a subject? Does it have a verb? Read the second part of the compound sentence. Does it have a subject? Does it have a verb? If you answered "yes," then it is a compound sentence.

Ex: The other lads looked up, and they smiled involuntarily.
The other lads looked up is a complete sentence.
They smiled involuntarily is a complete sentence.

Jeff saw a bear and ran back to his tent.
Jeff saw a bear is a complete sentence.
Ran back to his tent is <u>not</u> a complete sentence; there is no subject. This is not a compound sentence, therefore, do not use a comma. This sentence contains a compound verb. Jeff saw <u>and</u> ran.

3.
b.1) I ran the mile race, and John ran the hundred yard dash.
** 2) no comma needed**
** 3) I'm taking piano lessons, and Amy is taking guitar lessons.**

c. looked and smiled

d. and

b. Place commas correctly <u>if</u> it is a compound sentence.

   1) I ran the mile race and John ran the hundred yard dash.
   2) John competed in the hurdles and the shotput.
   3) I'm taking piano lessons and Amy is taking guitar lessons.

c. You learned in Lesson 22 that a conjunction is used to connect words that perform more than one function in a sentence. For example, in the first sentence of the literature passage, what two things do the lads do?

d. Circle the conjunction that joins these two verbs.

✎ **Teacher's Note: If your student has difficulty locating the subject and compound verb, tell him so he my continue with diagramming.**

e. Verbs connected in this way are called compound verbs and are diagrammed like this:

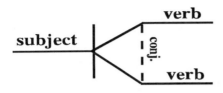

3.
f.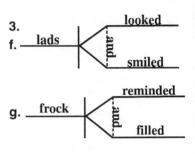

f. Diagram only the subject and the compound verb in this simplified sentence.

The other lads looked up and smiled involuntarily.

g.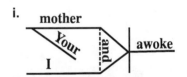

g. Diagram only the subject and the compound verb in this simplified sentence.

The black frock reminded them of her loss and filled the boyish hearts with a kindly desire.

h. Not only can a subject perform two or more actions, but two or more subjects can perform the same action. This is called a **compound subject** and is diagrammed like this:

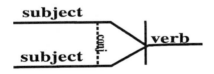

i. Look at the following sentence. Diagram every word.

Your mother and I awoke.

i.

(mother / Your / I and awoke)

j. Use your easy readers to find examples of compound subjects and compound verbs or identify these elements in the following sentences:
1) Hurriedly, Mary and Jim left the auditorium.
2) The red car and the blue van backed into each other.
3) The horse tugged and pulled the heavy load.
4) The naughty boy laughed at his mother and ran away.
5) The kitten and puppy slapped and nipped each other.

j. 1) Mary and Jim
    (compound subject)
2) car and van
    (compound subject)
3) tugged and pulled
    (compound verb)
4) laughed and ran
    (compound verb)
5) kitten and puppy
    (compound subject);
    slapped and nipped
    (compound verb)

4.
a. for

b. 1)

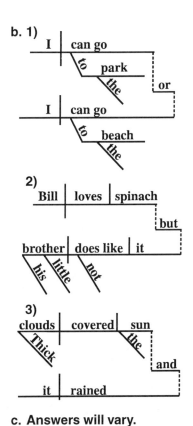

c. Answers will vary.

d.1) <u>Flying</u> vehicles amaze
    my grandmother.
  2) Jim put away his
    <u>folded</u> clothes.

4. a. Finally, not only can parts of a sentence be compounded, but sentences can as well. You know that a **simple sentence** consists of a subject and verb and makes one complete thought. That is, it can stand alone. Very often we connect two or more complete sentences to form a compound sentence. The first sentence in the literature passage is a compound sentence. Circle the conjunction joining the two complete sentences.

The main parts of a compound sentence would be diagrammed like this:

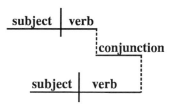

Notice that each sentence has its own base line. The second sentence is below the first, connected by the conjunction which is on a solid horizontal line.

b. Diagram the following compound sentences. By now, you should be able to diagram every word in the sentence.

1) I can go to the park, or I can go to the beach.
2) Bill loves spinach, but his little brother does not like it.
3) Thick clouds covered the sun, and it rained.

c. Do you remember the gerund? It is a verb form ending in **-ing** used as a noun. Write a sentence using a verb form as a gerund.

d. Look at the first sentence of the literature passage. The last two words read *laughing face*. In this sentence, the word *laughing* is a verb used as an adjective. This is called a **participle**. Participles are verb forms ending in **-ing** or **-ed** used as an adjective**.**
Ex: Her *bewildered* face surprised everyone.

Underline the participles.
1) Flying vehicles amaze my grandmother.
2) Jim put away his folded clothes.

e. Do not confuse a gerund with a participle. Read the following sentence. Is the italicized word a gerund or participle?

Emily loves jumping on the trampoline.

f. Review the direct objects in Lesson 12, **3c-g**. An action verb may also have two direct objects. A sentence with a compound direct object is diagrammed as follows:

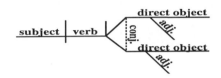

g. Look at the following sentence.

Homily knitted their jerseys and stockings.

Homily knitted what?

h. Diagram the subject, verb, adjective, and direct objects.

i. If you need to, review prepositions in Lesson 22, **2c-m**. A sentence may contain more than one prepositional phrase. Look at the diagram below.

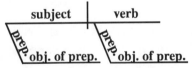

j. There can also be two or more objects of a preposition.

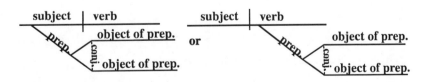

k. Find and diagram only the subject, verb, adjective, prepositional phrase, and predicate nominative in the following sentence. Look carefully, there are not only two objects but three.

The kinswoman was a winsome sight with her shy, soft eyes, bright hair, and laughing face.

4.

e. gerund

g. jerseys and stockings

h.

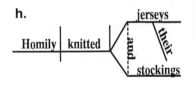

k.

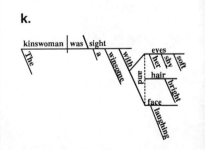

l. If you need to, review predicate adjectives and predicate nominatives in Lessons 10 and 17. A linking verb can have a compound predicate adjective or compound predicate nominative. They would be diagrammed as:

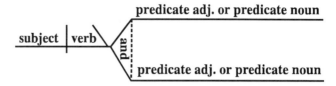

4.
m.

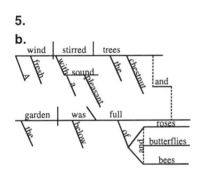

m. Diagram every word in the following sentence.

The evening was still and quiet and peaceful.

n. Optional: Take an oral or written spelling pretest.

5. a. Take the literature passage from dictation.
                        OR
    b. Diagram every word in the following sentence.

5.
b.

A fresh wind stirred the chestnut trees with a pleasant sound, and the garden below was full of roses, butterflies, and bees.
                        OR
    c. Choose skills from the *Review Activities* on the next page.

A final note: Being able to diagram sentences does not make you a better writer. Only actually writing can do that. Diagramming sentences helps you see the relationship between the parts of the sentence. You have probably discovered some sentences that you are still not sure how to diagram. When you run into these, just diagram the parts you are sure about. At a later date, you may wish to pursue a higher study of grammar. Sentence diagramming can be very complicated but a fun challenge!

Review Activities

Choose the skills your student needs to review.

1. *Compound Verb*
   Write a sentence with a compound verb.

2. *Compound Subject*
   Write a sentence with a compound subject.

3. *Compound Sentence*
   Join the two sentences with a conjunction to make a compound sentence. Choose the best conjunction, and don't forget the commas.

   a. Ronnie went mountain climbing. Steven stayed home.
   b. Sandy wrote a poem. It was published in a magazine.
   c. Today was good. Tomorrow will be better.
   d. Randy broke his arm. It is healed now.
   e. I like science fiction. My friend likes mysteries.

4. *Gerund*
   Write a sentence using a gerund.

5. *Participle*
   Write a sentence using a participle.

6. *Capitalization and Punctuation*
   Capitalize and punctuate.

   a. happy birthday mrs thompson exclaimed her students
   b. have you read a tale of two cities by charles dickens asked tom
   c. this week said casey let's run five miles
   d. what do you think asked uncle george
   e. my aunt said come back this spring

7. *Diagram (Compound Subject and Compound Verb, and Compound Sentence)*
   Diagram the sentences you wrote in 1-2. You may choose to diagram just the subject, verb, and conjunction.

---

1. Answers will vary.
   Ex: Jason mowed the yard and raked the leaves.
2. Answers will vary.
   Ex: Terry and her friends studied together.
3.
a. Ronnie went mountain climbing, and Steven stayed home.
b. Sandy wrote a poem, and it was published in a magazine.
c. Today was good, but tomorrow will be better.
d. Randy broke his arm, but it is healed now.
e. I like science fiction, but my friend likes mysteries.
4. Answers will vary.
   Ex: I enjoy *fishing*.
5. Answers will vary.
   Ex: Sarah rocked the *crying* baby.
6.
a. "Happy Birthday, Mrs. Thompson!" exclaimed her students.
b. "Have you read <u>A Tale of Two Cities</u> by Charles Dickens?" asked Tom.
c. "This week," said Casey, "let's run five miles."
d. "What do you think?" asked Uncle George.
e. My aunt said, "Come back this spring."

7. Answers will vary.

8.

a.

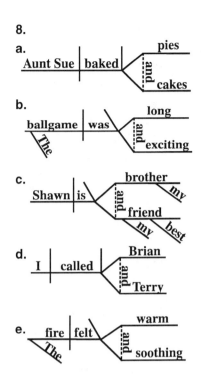

8. *Diagram (Compound Direct Object, Compound Predicate Adjective, and Compound Predicate Nominative)*
Diagram the sentences.

   a. Aunt Sue baked pies and cakes.
   b. The ballgame was long and exciting.
   c. Shawn is my brother and my best friend.
   d. I called Brian and Terry.
   e. The fire felt warm and soothing.

9. *Diagram (More than one prepositional phrase)*
Diagram the sentences.

   a. The boy with the lost dog walked around the corner.
   b. The book in the library was displayed for the students.
   c. The man at the window peered through the shades.

9.

a.

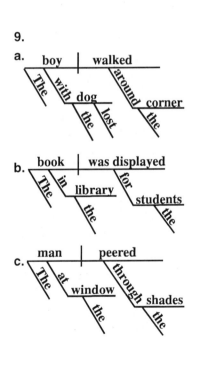

Assessment 7
(Lessons 22-23)

1. List five common prepositions.

2. Underline the prepositional phrases in the following sentences and tell if they are adjective phrases or adverb phrases:

    a. The neighbors across the street are moving.
    b. The baby slept in the crib.
    c. Peter jumped on the trampoline.
    d. The smile on the boy's face brightened the room.
    e. I talked to my brother.

3. Diagram the sentences above.

Continued on the next page.

---

1. Refer to Lesson 22.

2.
a. **across the street - adj. phrase**
b. **in the crib - adv. phrase**
c. **on the trampoline - adv. phrase**
d. **on the boy's face - adj. phrase**
e. **to my brother - adv. phrase**

3.
a.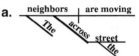

b.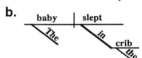

c.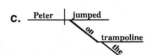

d.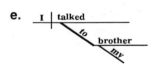

e.

4. Answers will vary, Ex:

a. <u>Mary and Martha</u> were
   sisters.

b. Martha <u>cleaned and
   cooked</u>.

c. She worked in the
   <u>kitchen and garden</u>.

d. Mary played the <u>piano
   and organ</u>.

5.

a.

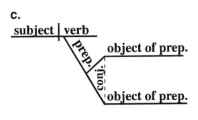

b.

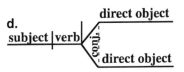

c.

d.

4. Write a sentence with:

   a. a compound subject
   b. a compound verb
   c. a compound object of a preposition
   d. a compound direct object

5. Draw the diagram form for each of the above.

BOOK STUDY

on

Adam and His Kin

Adam and His Kin

Adam and His Kin
by Dr. Ruth Beechick
Published by Arrow Press

Readability level: 7th grade

Summary

Subtitled "The Lost History of Their Lives and Times," *Adam and His Kin* is a simple retelling of the events in the first chapters of Genesis filled out with information culled from the research of Dr. Ruth Beechick. She brings her imagination to the narrative to describe what each person might have said or done.

Dr. Beechick carefully follows the timeline of Scripture, detailing each day of Creation and the crime and punishment of Adam and Eve. It is at this point that the story takes on a new freshness as Dr. Beechick brings together information from many sources which include archeology, astronomy, ancient traditions and religions, as well as the Bible itself.

Plausible answers are given to many age old questions such as how mankind learned language, how skills were developed, and who kept alive the memory of the distant past as Dr. Beechick tells the story of the Old Testament Patriarchs from Adam to Abram. In Dr. Beechick's own words:

At first I wrote that 'maybe' Adam and Eve walked in the garden on their first day, 'perhaps' they enjoyed the flowers, and so forth. Later, I realized that I couldn't annoy my readers with 'maybe' all through the story. So I have decided to say one big 'maybe' here in the preface and hope that will suffice.

1-5.   a. The book you will read and base your research and writing on during this four week unit is *Adam and His Kin* by Dr. Ruth Beechick. This book is a simple narrative of the first eleven chapters of Genesis. In addition to the Bible, Dr. Beechick has gathered her information from many sources including astronomy, archaeology, and ancient traditions and religions.

       b. This week, read Genesis chapters 1 - 11, and then begin reading *Adam and His Kin*.

1-5. a. Continue in your reading of *Adam and His Kin*.

b. Reading *Adam and His Kin* may have given you a fresh look at the first eleven chapters of Genesis. Maybe it answered some questions you had or made you think of new questions.

c. Write out some questions you still don't know the answers to. Take the time to do some independent research to try to find some of the answers. Begin by discussing your questions with your teacher. You might set up an appointment with your pastor to ask him the questions. Next, stop by the church library to look for books and commentaries that might help.

d. Write a brief report about one or more of the topics you looked into.

1-5.   a. As Christians we believe that the world and all it contains
            was created by God.

*In the beginning God created the heavens and the
earth.*
                                        Genesis 1:1 (NASB)

*'Ah Lord GOD! Behold, Thou hast made the heavens
and the earth by Thy great power and by Thine
outstretched arm! Nothing is too difficult for thee.*
                                        Jeremiah 32:17 (NASB)

*O Lord, it is Thou who DIDST MAKE THE HEAVEN
AND THE EARTH AND THE SEA, AND ALL THAT IS
IN THEM.*
                                        Acts 4:24 (NASB)

Read one or more books by authors who defend this
creationist view. Some books are suggested below. If
these seem difficult to read, try scanning the tables of
contents to find chapters that have the information you're
looking for.

*The Genesis Record, The Biblical Basis for Modern
Science, The Bible has the Answer*, all by Dr. Henry M.
Morris

*The Controversy - Roots of the Creation-Evolution
Conflict* by Donald E. Chittick

Unlocking the Mysteries of Creation by Dennis R.
Petersen or any other appropriate books

    b. Talk to your teacher about what you are reading. Does
        your teacher agree with what the books say? Interview
        your pastor. What has he found in his studies? Maybe
        you know other grown-ups who would like to talk about
        these topics. If you talk to an evolutionist, find out what
        you can about his beliefs.

    c. Write a theme explaining the evolutionary belief and the
        creationist belief. This could be a large assignment, but
        try to summarize a few points about each view, and
        mention a few of the major problems. Write a concluding
        paragraph stating your belief and why you think the way
        you do.

The most common form of the development of a **theme** is the deductive form, where you have two or three items to discuss which deal with your main idea. The first paragraph will contain a generalization (**thesis statement**) of the items. In this case the statement will tell the two views you will be reporting on. For example:

There are two major views held about the origin of life.

The thesis statement will then be put into an opening paragraph:

How did life begin? This is a question that most people attempt to answer at some time. There are two major views held about the origin of life. I believe it is important to understand these views in order to better answer this question.

Your next two paragraphs will go on to describe both of the views, what is believed, and any major problems with the view. Finally, the last paragraph should contain your conclusion and why you have come to it.

d. In addition to or instead of the theme on evolution versus Creation, you could write about two kinds of creationists. One kind, like the authors listed above, believe in a young earth. That means that God created the earth only a few thousand years ago -- maybe about 6000 years, or not more than 10,000 years ago. The other kind believe in an old earth -- that God created the earth millions of years ago. If you talk to or read an old earth creationist, learn what you can about his or her beliefs. Then write a theme describing the differences between the young earth and old earth views. Again, write a concluding paragraph stating your belief and why you think the way you do. In both themes it will be all right to state that you're not yet sure of your beliefs, and that you want to read and study more before you make up your mind.

But sanctify the Lord God in your hearts: and be ready always to give an answer to every man that asketh you a reason of the hope that is in you with meekness and fear.

I Peter 3:15 (KJV)

The Writing Process

A. Begin the theme

- Ask a question and then state that you intend to answer it.
- Use a pertinent quotation from a book, an authority, etc.
- State your topic.
- Begin with a dependent clause: When you think about it... Although most people don't know...

B. Connect the parts

- When similiar points are being made use **transitional words** and phrase connectives: While... moreover... to sum up... furthermore.
- When contrasting points are being made use transitional words and phrase connectives: nonetheless... despite this... on the other hand... however.
- To indicate stages in your argument use transitional words: initially... at the onset... to begin with... in condition... lastly... finally.
- Number your division using transitional words: the first... a second... in the third place...
- Use parallel sentence structure:
  The Bible explains God's relationship to man.
  The Bible explains man's relationship to God.
  The Bible explains man's relationship to man.

C. End the theme

- with a pertinent question.
- by repeating your opening topic.
- with a personal opinion, additional information, a warning, or a declaration of intent.

D. Proofread

- Title - Capitalize main words.
- Format - neatness, margins, etc.
- Check spelling.
- Check for complete sentences.
- Check for problem words: its-it's, whose-who's, theirs-there's, accept-except, affect-effect, to-too, lose-loose, chose-choose.

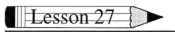

Teacher's Note:
Sometimes the spelling of biblical names varies from one translation to another. The King James Version was used in this section.

1. a. Compare a chapter in *Adam and His Kin* with its biblical reference in Genesis. Notice how closely Dr. Beechick is relating the Genesis account in "story form." This is called **narration**.

   b. *Adam and His Kin* tells the story through Genesis 11. Read Genesis 12. Following Dr. Beechick's style, try writing the next chapter using what you have just read in Genesis 12. You may use just the Bible or you might like to try drawing some additional information from another source, such as a Christian history book. For example, you could look up Egypt and find out what it was like during this time to help you describe the scene better.

   c. Optional: If you enjoy this exercise, write a narration of the next chapter of Genesis or another portion of the Bible. Do this on a separate sheet of paper.

   d. Use *Student Activity Book* Lesson 27, Chart A, or follow these directions to make your own chart. Referring back to Genesis 5, 9:29, 11, 25:7, 35:28, and 47:28, make a list of all the men mentioned. Next to each man's name record each man's birth date, death date, and age at death. Your list should include 22 men from Adam through Jacob. With the data tabulated in this form you may observe some trends. (Keep this record; you will add information in **4a**.)

2. a. It has been said that a picture is worth a thousand words. As a researcher and writer you will find there will be times when it will be more helpful to present your information in picture form. A **graph** is a picture used to present facts so that they will be clearer and easier to understand. It is usually easier to draw conclusions or make comparisons from items illustrated in a graph than to try to figure out columns of figures or paragraphs of facts.

1. d. Answer

Chart A

Bible Character	Birth Date	Death Date	Age at Death	Age at Son's Birth
Adam	0	930	930	130
Seth	130	1042	912	105
Enos	235	1140	905	90
Cainan	325	1235	910	70
Mahalaleel	395	1290	895	65
Jared	460	1422	962	162
Enoch	622	987	365	65
Methuseleh	687	1656	969	187
Lamech	874	1651	777	182
Noah	1056	2006	950	500
Shem	1556	2158	600	100
Arphaxad	1658	2096	438	35
Salah	1693	2126	433	30
Eber	1723	2187	464	34
Peleg	1757	1996	239	30
Reu	1787	2026	239	32
Serug	1819	2049	230	30
Nahor	1849	1997	148	29
Terah	1878	2083	205	130
Abraham	2008	2183	175	100
Isaac	2108	2288	180	60
Jacob	2168	2315	174	

b. A **line graph** is one of the simplest types of graphs. The line shows the relationship between two variables or parameters. For example, it can be used to show how a man's life expectancy changed from the time of Adam to the time of Abraham.

Use *Student Activity Book* Lesson 27, chart B, or a sheet of graph paper, or quadrille ruled paper (4 squares to the inch). Lay out horizontal (**x**) and vertical (**y**) axis for your line graph. The scale of your **x** and **y** axis will determine how large your chart is. Use 1/4" spacing for each man's name (or whatever is convenient on your graph paper). The names of the men should go on the **x** axis, along the bottom. You may need to turn the names vertical under the axis to fit them in the 1/4" spacing.

c. Observing that the oldest man lived 969 years, you may want to mark off your **x** axis 0 to 1000 years. Mark off every 100 years using 1/2" spacing for each 100 years. Label this axis "Age at Death."

d. Now that you have created your chart axis, put a small dot or an **x** above each man's name, at the location corresponding to his age at death, and connect the dots (or **x**'s) with a line. Your chart is complete except for any titles or explanations you may wish to add.

Trends that you may have noticed before in the tabulated data should be more pronounced using the line graph.

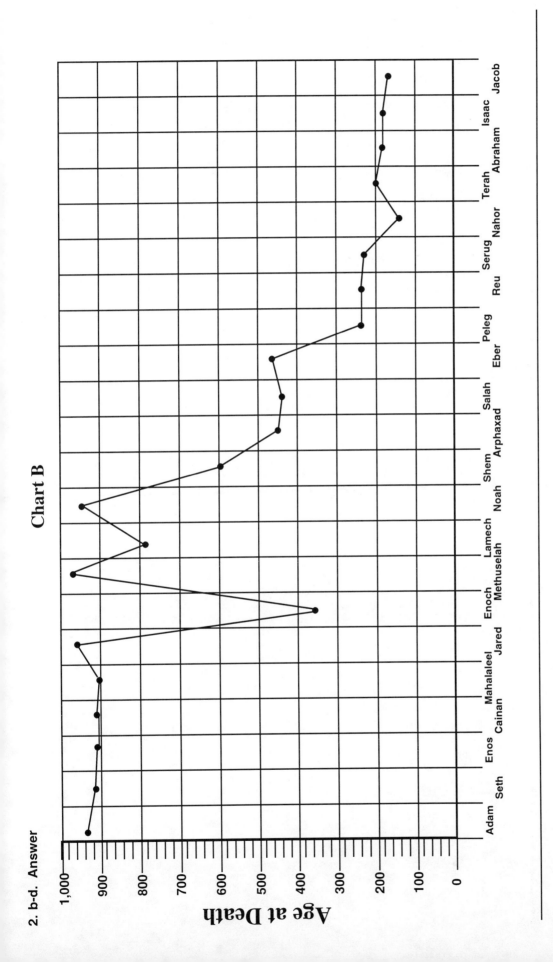

Chart B

2. b-d. Answer

3. a. A **bar graph** also can be used to illustrate trends in your data. A bar graph uses vertical or horizontal bars to make comparisons. Use *Student Activity Book* Lesson 27, Chart C, or follow these directions for a vertical bar graph. Prepare your graph as you did for the line graph. Instead of dots or **x**'s marking each man's age, draw a rectangle, or "bar," that extends from the **x** axis to the point marking the man's age at death.

3. a. Answer

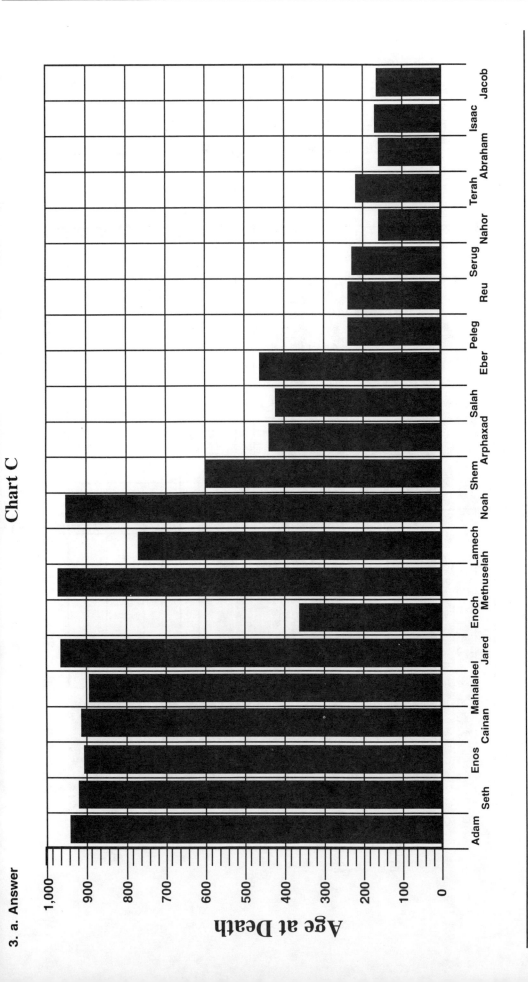

Chart C

Age at Death

1,000 900 800 700 600 500 400 300 200 100 0

Adam Seth Enos Cainan Mahalaleel Jared Enoch Methuselah Lamech Noah Shem Arphaxad Salah Eber Peleg Reu Serug Nahor Terah Abraham Isaac Jacob

b. Use *Student Activity Book* Lesson 27, Chart D, or follow these directions for a horizontal bar graph. A horizontal bar graph could also be created by exchanging the **x** and **y** axis. Starting on the **y** axis, with Adam at the top, list the 22 men. The **x** axis would then be marked off for 1000 years. Drawing the bars from left to right gives you a horizontal bar graph.

3. b. Answer

Chart D

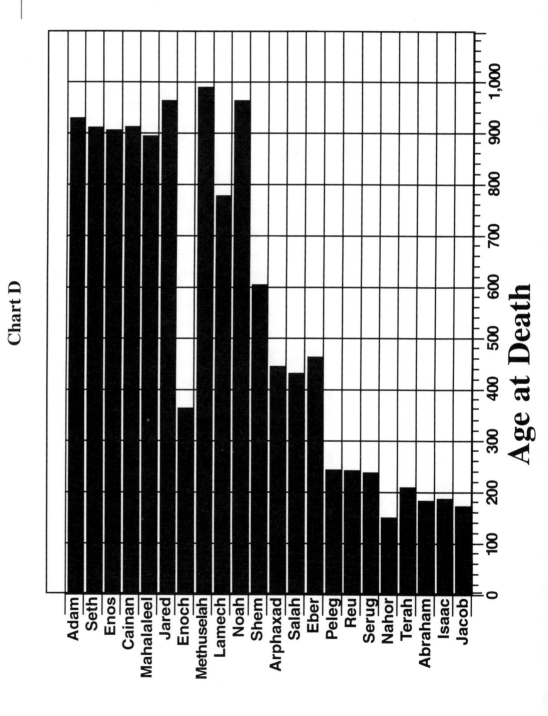

4. a. Another interesting study is how the lives of the earliest humans overlapped. Did you know that Noah's grandfather, Methuselah, could have known Adam for over 200 years? You can show this information by making a timeline. You've already created a table of ages for the 22 Bible characters. On this same table or using Chart A again, add each man's age when his son was born.

b. Create a larger graph area by taping three sheets of graph paper together end-to-end so that the grid spacing is maintained from sheet to sheet. Turn your paper sideways, draw a line 30" long, 1" from the bottom. Mark this line for 2500 years, with each inch representing 100 years. On the left hand side of the sheet list the 22 men, with Adam at the bottom.

c. Now draw a line, or a bar (your choice), next to Adam's name, extending from his time of birth to his death. This line should extend from 1 to 930. From Genesis 5:3, you can see that Seth's line should begin at 130, and verse 8 tells you how long to make it. Calculate birth and death dates for each of the other men and mark your chart accordingly. Shem and Abram are not so easy to figure as the others. Here are verses to help you. Shem: Genesis 11:32 and 12:4, along with Acts 7:4, contain information for figuring the age of Terah when Abram was born. Abraham was much younger than his brother Haran.

Ex:

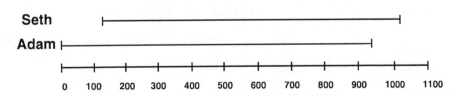

4.
b-c. Answer on next page.

d. You now have a timeline which starts with the year 0 at the creation of the world. But what year was that using our present dating system? A good Bible handbook, dictionary, or atlas will give you an approximate date for Abraham. You can then write dates relative to our system under your original dates.

5. One last type of graph you can work with is the **family tree**. Look at the family trees Dr. Beechick worked out for you in *Adam and His Kin* on pages 43 and 61. These family trees basically follow one line of descendants. Draw a family tree, either for your family, by asking your parents, grandparents, aunts, and uncles for information; or for someone else that you know by interviewing their family members.

4.

b-c. Answer
     **The graph is scaled
     down**

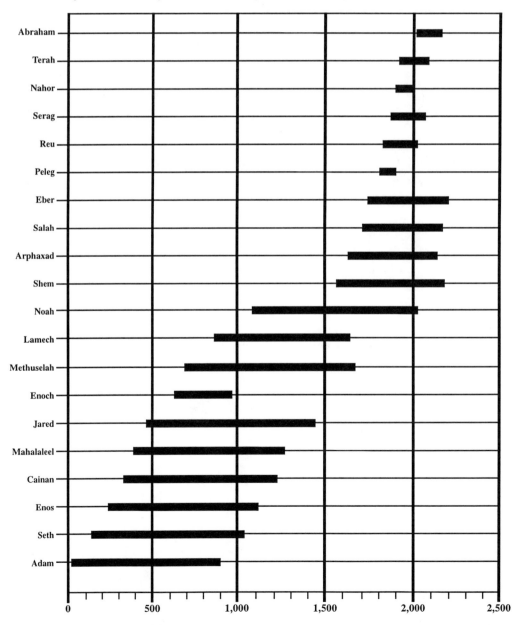

Assessment 8
(Lessons 24 - 27)

1. What transitional words may be used to connect similiar points?

2. What transitional words may be used to connect contrasting points?

3. What transitional words may be used to indicate stages in your argument?

4. What transitional words may be used to number your division?

5. What is narration?

6. Name two types of graphs.

1. while, moreover, to sum up, furthermore.

2. nonetheless, despite this, on the other hand, however

3. initially, at the onset, to begin with, in condition

4. the first, a second, in the third place

5. a retelling in story form

6. bar graph, line graph

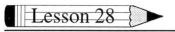

✎ **Teacher's Note:** As your student completes this lesson, choose skills from the _Review Activties_ that he needs. The _Review Activities_ follow this lesson.

Blessed is the man who shuns the place
Where sinners love to meet;
Who fears to tread their wicked ways,
And hates the scoffer's seat;

But in the statutes of the Lord
Hath placed his chief delight;
By day he reads or hears the Word,
And meditates by night.

He like a plant of generous kind,
By living waters set,
Safe from the storms and blasting wind,
Enjoys a peaceful state.

Green as the leaf and ever fair
Shall his profession shine,
While fruits of holiness appear
Like clusters on the vine.

Not so the impious and unjust;
What vain designs they form!
Their hopes are blown away like dust,
Or chaff before the storm.

Sinners in judgment shall not stand
Amongst the sons of grace,
When Christ the Judge, at His right hand
Appoints His saints a place.

His eye beholds the path they tread,
His heart approves it well;
But crooked ways of sinners lead
Down to the gates of hell.

"Psalm 1" _by Isaac Watts_

✎ **Teacher's Note:** Omit title when reading to your student.

1. a. Listen as your teacher reads this poem by Isaac Watts. Is the poem familiar to you?

   b. Copy the poem or take one verse from dictation. In this poem, each new line is capitalized even though it does not always begin a new sentence.

There are many styles in poetry writing, and sometimes poets prefer not to capitalize the first word of a line.

c. Proofread carefully and correct any errors in punctuation, or spelling. Make a spelling list to study this week or use the following suggested words: scoff, tread, holiness, profession.

d. When you spell a word ending in **f**, **l**, **s**, or **z** at the end of a word, you often double the letter.

> ### Spelling Tip
> One syllable root words ending in **f, l, s,** and **z** are often doubled at the end of a word. Ex: scoff; scoffer

e. Write the following words, and underline the double consonants. Say the words aloud as you write them.

mill	huff	kiss	buzz
bell	mess	fill	chaff

f. All words referring to God (including pronouns) and the Bible are capitalized.
Ex: Word of God, Prince of Peace, Son of God, He

Find all the words in the literature passage which refer to God and the Bible.

g. Capitalize the sentences.
  1) god's word is nourishment for the soul.
  2) i find comfort in knowing he (God) is with me.
  3) god shines his love on everyone.

1.
f. Lord, Word, Christ the Judge, His right hand, His saints, His eye, His heart

g.1) God's Word is nourishment for the soul.
  2) I find comfort in knowing He (God) is with me.
  3) God shines His love on everyone.

2. a. When adding **-ness, -ment, -less, -er, -est,** or **-ed** to words ending in **y**, preceded by a consonant, change the **y** to **i** before adding the suffix. When adding **-ing** to words ending in **y**, keep the **y.**

> ## Spelling Tip
> When adding a suffix to words ending in a consonant and **y**, like **holy**, change the **y** to **i** before adding **-er, -est, -ness, -ment,** or **-less**. Keep the **y** when adding **-ing.**

b. Complete the chart.

	-ness -ment -less	-er -est -ed
Ex: holy	holiness	holier, holiest
1) happy		
2) lovely		
3) empty		
4) merry		

c. Read Psalm 1 in the Bible. Compare it to Isaac Watts' poem. How closely does Mr. Watts follow the Scripture?

d. What is the rhyme scheme of this poem? What is its rhythmic foot? Refer to *The Poetry Unit*, lesson 7, if you don't remember.

e. Find an example of a simile in the passage. Refer to *The Poetry Unit* Lesson 5 if you need to review similes.

f. If you have a hymnal available, look through it to find other poems that Isaac Watts wrote that have been set to music.

3. a. You have learned about a gerund and participle. Another way a verb form may be used is as an **infinitive**. An infinitive is formed with the word *to* before the word. Infinitives are usually used as a noun or adjective.
Ex: **To run** a marathon is a great feat. (noun)
    The man **to run** the marathon is Mark. (adjective)

2.
b.1) happiness
   happier, happiest
2) loveliness
   lovelier, loveliest
3) emptiness
   emptied
4) merriment
   merrier, merriest

c. Answers will vary.

d. abab
   trochaic

e. He like a plant
   Green as the leaf
   fruits of holiness appear
   Like clusters
   hopes are blown away like dust

f. Answers will vary according to your hymnal.

b. Underline the infinitive.
   1) Jesse will learn to bake.
   2) The pie to make is Jerry's recipe.

c. Write a sentence using an infinitive.

d. Begin memorizing this version of Psalm 1 by Isaac Watts.

e. Using a favorite psalm, begin writing a poem about it just as Mr. Watts has done with Psalm l.

f. Review your spelling words.

4. a. Continue your memorization work.

   b. Finish writing your poem.

   c. Write a sentence using an infinitive.

   d. Look at the first verse in the passage. Why is *scoffer's* spelled with an apostrophe **s** (**'s**)? Write the plural possessive for "the seats belonging to the scoffers."

   e. Optional: Take an oral or written spelling pretest.

5. a. Write Isaac Watts' "Psalm 1" from memory.
                          OR
   b. Take it from dictation once again.
                          OR
   c. Choose skills from the *Review Activities* on the next page.

3.
b.1) Jesse will learn <u>to bake.</u>
  2) The pie <u>to make</u> is Jerry's recipe.

c. Answers will vary.

4.
c. Answers will vary.
  Ex: I like *to read*.

d. To show a possessive form, an apostrophe s ('s) is used.
scoffers' seats

1.

a.

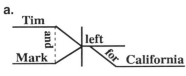

b.

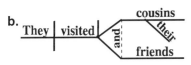

c.

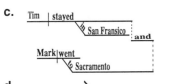

d.

e.

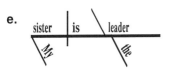

2. Answers will vary.
   Ex: Matt sang and
   danced around the room.

3. Answers will vary.
   Ex: Jill and I walked
   home.

4. Answers will vary.
   Ex: The phone rang, so I
   answered it.

5.
a. Wow, the car show in
   Atlanta, Georgia was
   great!
b. Paula was born on
   September 3, 1985.
c. My aunt's dog had five
   black and white puppies.
d. Mom, have you seen
   Karen's bookbag?
e. Mom said, "I think it's in
   Tom's room."
f. Jesus is the Prince of
   Peace.

Review Activities

Choose the skills your student needs to review.

1. *Diagram*
   Diagram every word in the following sentences.
   a. Tim and Mark left for California.
   b. They visited their cousins and friends.
   c. Tim stayed in San Fransico, and Mark went to Sacramento.
   d. Dinner smells delicious.
   e. My sister is the leader.

2. *Compound Verb*
   Write a sentence with a compound verb.

3. *Compound Subject*
   Write a sentence with a compound subject.

4. *Compound Sentence*
   Write a compound sentence.

5. *Capitalization and Punctuation*
   Add capitalization and punctuation.

   a. wow the car show in atlanta georgia was great
   b. paula was born on september 3 1985
   c. my aunts dog had five black and white puppies
   d. mom have you seen karens bookbag
   e. mom said I think its in toms room
   f. jesus is the prince of peace

6. *Simile*
   Write a sentence using a simile.

7. *Gerund, participle, infinitive*
   Write three sentences using a gerund, participle, and infinitive.

8. *Plurals (Irregular)*
   The fourth verse of the literature passage refers to "green as the leaf." Write the plural form for *leaf.*

---

6. **Answers will vary.**
   Ex: Her eyes twinkled like little stars.

7. **Answers will vary.**
   Ex:
   gerund-*Jogging* is good exercise.
   participle-He waved to the *screaming* fans.
   infinitive-The man *to run* the marathon is Mark.

8. **leaves**

Edith Nesbit (1858 - 1924) was 40 years old when she wrote the first book about the Bastable children, *The Story of the Treasure Seekers,* in order to raise money for her family. As an adult, Mrs. Nesbit was a nonconformist, shocking the society of her day by cutting her hair short and smoking. In writing about the Bastables, however, she drew from her very conventional English upbringing. For instance, the games the Bastable children play are taken from memories of her own young life. Critics say that her books are among the first to talk to children, not as miniature men and women, but for what they are.

I am afraid the last chapter was rather dull. It is always dull in books when people talk and talk, and don't do anything, but I was obliged to put it in, or else you wouldn't have understood all the rest. The best part of books is when things are happening. That is the best part of real things too. This is why I shall not tell you in this story about all the days when nothing happened. You will not catch me saying, 'thus the sad days passed slowly by' - or ' the years rolled on their weary course' - or ' time went on' - because it is silly; of course time goes on - whether you say so or not. So I shall just tell you the nice, interesting parts - and in between you will understand that we had our meals and got up and went to bed, and dull things like that.

The Story of the Treasure Seekers by E. Nesbit

1. a. Take the literature passage from dictation. Write only the bolded section.

   b. Proofread and make any necessary corrections. Make a spelling list to study this week or use the following suggested list: obliged, happened, whether, interesting.

   > ### Spelling Tip
   > Words like **happen** are spelled with a double consonant to keep the short vowel sound of **a**.

   c. Circle the correctly spelled words.
      1) a meal   supper   super
      2) fantastic   supper   super
      3) a meal   dinner   diner
      4) a restaurant   dinner   diner

1.
c. 1) supper
**   2) super**
**   3) dinner**
**   4) diner**

2. a. You will remember that a pronoun is a word that takes the place of a noun. For this lesson, refer to the Personal Pronoun Chart found in Lesson 1. Pronouns can indicate several things.

   b. Pronouns can be either singular or plural. Can you think of an example of each?

   c. Pronouns can also show possession. Give an example of a possessive pronoun.

   d. Pronouns can be subjects or objects in a sentence. List all the subjective and objective pronouns.

   e. When referring to another person and yourself as the subject, use the subjective pronoun, *I.*
       Ex: Jason and I played ball. (correct)
           Jason and me played ball. (incorrect)

       An easy way to find the correct pronoun is to say the sentence without the other subject.
       Ex: I played ball. (By omitting *Jason,* the sentence sounds correct.)
           Me played ball. (By omitting *Jason,* the sentence sounds incorrect.)

       The above rule is the same with objective pronouns.
       Ex: Casey threw the ball to Jason and I. (incorrect)
           Say to yourself, "Casey threw the ball to I."
           It sounds incorrect.
           Casey threw the ball to Jason and me. (correct)
           Say to yourself, "Casey threw the ball to me."
           It sounds correct.

       Note also, like opening the door for someone and letting him in first, it is best to name yourself last.

   f. Circle the correct pronouns. Use the pronoun test above.

       1) Yesterday, Karla and (I, *me*) went to the theater.
       2) The tickets belong to Karla and (*I, me*).
       3) At the theater, Karla and (I, *me*) saw Jenny.

2.

b. Refer to Pronoun Chart in Lesson 1.

c. Refer to Pronoun Chart in Lesson 1.

d. I, you, he, she, it, they, we (subjective pronouns) me, you, him, her, it, them, us (objective pronouns)

f. 1) I
   2) me
   3) I

2.
h. first person

i. predicate adjective

✏ **Teacher's Note: Some grammar books refer to these words as homophones.**

3.
b. 1) to
**   2) two**
**   3) too**

d. *To bed* **is a prepositional phrase.**

g. Finally, pronouns indicate whether the person is speaking, is spoken to, or is spoken about. A **first person pronoun** is used in place of the name of the speaker (i.e., I). A **second person pronoun** is used to name the person or thing spoken to (i.e., you). A **third person pronoun** is used to name the person or thing spoken about (i.e., he). Refer to the Personal Pronoun Chart in Lesson 1.

h. Is the literature passage written in the first, second, or third person?

i. Look at the first two sentences in the literature passage. What kind of word is *dull* in this sentence? Review predicate adjectives in Lesson 17 if you don't remember.

3. a. Say the following words aloud.

        to   too   two

Words that sound alike but are spelled differently and have different meanings are called **homonyms**. *To, too,* and *two* are homonyms. Underline the words *to* and *too* in the literature passage. Each one of these words acts as a different part of speech. *Too* is an adverb. The word *to* joins with the word following it to form a **phrase** (a connected group of words that act as a unit). *Two* is a number, therefore it is an adjective.

b. Choose the correct word.
    1) The man walked (*to, too, two*) the gate.
    2) He saw (*to, too, two*) apple trees.
    3) He saw a cherry tree, (*to, too, two*).

c. In the second sentence of the literature passage, circle the phrase *to put*. In the last sentence of the literature passage, circle the phrase *to bed*. Whenever the word, *to* is followed by a noun or pronoun which answers the questions *to whom* or *to what,* it is acting as a preposition.

d. Which one of the two phrases is a prepositional phrase:

            to put   OR   to bed

If you need to review prepositions, refer to Lesson 22, **2c-m**.

e. What part of speech is the word *put*? Do you remember that a phrase beginning with the word *to* and followed by a verb is called an infinitive? An infinitive is usually used as a noun or adjective.

f. Refer to the literature passage in Lessons 1 and 2, and practice identifying the word *to*. Is it used as a preposition or as an infinitive? Remember, the word *to* in a prepositional phrase will be followed by a noun or pronoun answering the questions *to whom* or *to what*? The word *to* in an infinitive will be followed by a verb.

g. Review your spelling words.

4. a. Do you think the writer of the literature passage is stating a fact or his opinion?

b. What is a fact?

c. What is an opinion? If you are not sure, look in the dictionary.

d. What kind of book do you like the best? Write a paragraph of three to five sentences giving your opinion and telling why you think so. Use examples.

e. Optional: Take an oral or written spelling pretest.

5. a. Read and edit the paragraph you wrote yesterday.
OR
b. Take the literature passage from dictation again.
OR
c. Choose skills from the *Review Activities* on the next page.

3.
e. verb

f. to the house
   (prepositional)
   to make (infinitive)
   to me (preposition)
   to know (infinitive)
   to do (infinitive)
   to know (infinitive)

4.
a. opinion

b. something true that can be proven
c. a personal feeling or belief

d. Answers will vary.

Review Activities

Choose the skills your student needs to review.

1.
a. infinitive
b. participle
c. gerund

1. *Gerund, Participle, Infinitive*
   Read the following sentences. Tell if the italicized words are gerunds, participles, or infinitives.

   a. Early in the morning, I sit on the beach *to meditate*.
   b. The *defeated* team trudged into the locker room.
   c. *Running* is good exercise.

2.
a. I
b. me
c. me
d. me
e. I

2. *Pronoun*
   Use the correct pronoun to complete these sentences. (I or me)

   a. My brother and ___ play hockey.
   b. Robert came with Jesse and ___.
   c. They were suprised to see Eric and ___ at the museum.
   d. Sam always follows Mike and ___.
   e. Whenever mom needs help, Kelly and ___ are always there.

3.
a. too
b. to
c. to
d. two
e. too

3. *Homonym*
   Use the correct homonym: to two too.

   a. We would like to come, ___.
   b. I have ___ leave soon.
   c. I hope ___ see you there.
   d. We saw ___ bald eagles.
   e. She arrived ___ late.

BOOK STUDY

on the play
Much
Ado About
Nothing

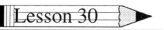

**Much Ado About Nothing,
a play by William
Shakespeare**

**Published by Signet
Classics or Folger Library**

**For your convenience, we
have included the synopsis
of *Much Ado About
Nothing* taken from *Tales
from Shapespeare* by
Charles and Mary Lamb.
You will find this at the end
of Lesson 32.**

Tales from Shakespeare - Charles (1775-1834) and Mary (1764-1847)
Lamb. Charles Lamb became famous as a literary critic and essayist. He
was noted for his warmth and sense of humor. As an adult, Charles had the
guardianship of his sister Mary, who suffered bouts of insanity. When
normal, she was described as intelligent and affectionate. With Charles, she
authored three books for children. The best known is *Tales from
Shakespeare*, the retelling of stories of Shakespeare's plays in which
Charles wrote the tragedies and Mary wrote the comedies.

For this *Book Study*, you will need to visit your library and
check out the play, *Much Ado About Nothing,* or purchase a copy
from the bookstore. We recommend the play published by
Signet Classics or the Folger Library. Both have helpful
footnotes. It is written in play form, divided into five acts with
two to five scenes in each act. The following three lessons
contain excerpts from the play.

Students have long studied Shakespeare's writings. Many
benefits may be gained from such a study. His writings are
universally recognized as classics. After the Bible, he has
probably had the most influence on western literature. We quote
him frequently without even knowing it. In addition, there are
countless literary allusions made to Shakespeare's work.

Another benefit of studying Shakespeare's writings is the
appreciation your student will acquire for good language. The
works of Shakespeare are akin to classical music in that the
complexity and beauty require the listener to exercise his
attention in order to enjoy them fully. It has been proven that
listening to classical music can temporarily elevate a person's
I.Q. Likewise, reading and enjoying Shakespeare will cause
your student to think.

Controversy may arise from the fact that Shakespeare wrote
about delicate subjects. In addition, his humor can be very crude
at times. Taking this into consideration, we feel that the study of
Shakespeare has a place in a quality language arts program.
Many of the objectionable comments may not be understood by
your student and it will be up to you to pass by them or discuss
them. As always, it is recommended that you be familiar with
the literature you are teaching. This way there will be no
surprises.

They found they had both been tricked into a belief of love, which had never existed, and had become lovers in truth by the power of a false jest: but the affection, which a merry invention had cheated them into, was grown too powerful to be shaken by a serious explanation; and since Benedick proposed to marry, he was resolved to think nothing to the purpose that the world could say against it; and he merrily kept up the jest, and swore to Beatrice, that he took her but for pity, and because he heard she was dying of love for him; and Beatrice protested, that she yielded but upon great persuasion, and partly to save his life, for she heard he was in a consumption. So these two mad wits were reconciled, and made a match of it.

Tales from Shakespeare by Charles and Mary Lamb

1. a. Listen as your teacher reads the literature passage.

   b. This paragraph is from a very special book written by a brother and sister, Charles and Mary Lamb. It was published in 1807 and is the retelling of twenty of William Shakespeare's tragedies and comedies. The book was intended to introduce children to the works of Shakespeare, but adults find it very helpful, too.

   Discuss with your teacher why Charles and Mary Lamb would think it helpful to retell Shakespeare's plays.

1.
b. There are several reasons it is helpful to retell Shakespeare's plays. Here are three:

   1) The plots are very often so intricate they are difficult to follow at one reading. A synopsis helps to simplify this.
   2) The language and sentence structure is very different from ours and makes it difficult to understand easily.
   3) The meanings of some words have changed or the words have completely fallen out of use.

1.

c. mad - merry
   wits - people who are
   amusingly clever

d. *Much Ado About*
   Nothing **is a comedy.**

3.

b. Hero - daughter of
   Leonato, cousin of
   Beatrice
   Beatrice - niece of
   Leonato, cousin of Hero
   Leonato - governor of
   Messina, Hero's father
   Don Pedro - prince of
   Arragon
   Claudio - a lord of
   Florence, in love with
   Hero
   Benedick -   a lord of
   Padua
   Ursula - a gentlewoman,
   Hero's attendant
   Margaret - a
   gentlewoman, Hero's
   attendant
   Don John -   Don Pedro's
   half-brother
   Borachio - a follower of
   Don John

c. The literature passage is part of the retelling of *Much Ado About Nothing*. Discuss the passage with your teacher. If you don't understand some of the words, look them up. For instance, what does "these two mad wits" mean?

d. Shakespeare's plays have elements of comedy and tragedy. Generally, a play is considered a **comedy** if it has a happy ending and a **tragedy** if it has a sad ending. Do you think the play this is from is a tragedy or a comedy?

2. a. Over the next few weeks you will be reading the play *Much Ado About Nothing* by Shakespeare. William Shakespeare is considered to be the greatest playwright the world has ever known and perhaps the finest English speaking poet in history.

   Optional: Check out a book of quotes from Shakespeare from the library. You will be surprised at how many of his words and phrases are a part of our everyday language, such as "in one fell swoop" and "wild-goose chase."

b. The problem with reading Shakespeare is that language has changed since his time. Some words are hard to understand because their meanings have changed or they are no longer even in use. To overcome this problem read his work out loud, then discuss it with someone, and always have a dictionary nearby. Today, begin our study by reading the synopsis of *Much Ado About Nothing*, found at the end of Lesson 32.

3. a. Before you actually begin reading the play *Much Ado About Nothing*, find out a little information about the life and times of William Shakespeare. The encyclopedia is a good place to start. There you will probably find a shorter synopsis of *Much Ado About Nothing*. It will help you to become as familiar as you can with the plot.

b. Review the synopsis of the play you read yesterday. This time make a list of the characters mentioned and who they are, especially noting their relationship to others in the story.

4. a. Today you will begin reading the play, *Much Ado About Nothing*. It is written in play form, divided into five acts with two to five scenes in each act. Read Act I, Scene I. Refer to the list of characters you made yesterday until you are familiar with each one's role.

b. What is the relationship between Leonato and Don Pedro? Between Claudio and Benedick? Between Claudio and Hero? Between Benedick and Beatrice?

c. What does Don Pedro hope to do for Claudio?

Continued on next page...

4.

b. Leonato is pleased to greet Don Pedro: "Never came trouble to my house in the likeness of your grace; for trouble being gone, comfort should remain; but when you depart from me, sorrow abides, and happiness takes his leave."

Claudio and Benedick are good friends: "He is most in the company of the right noble Claudio."

Claudio admires Hero "In mine eye, she is the sweetest lady that ever I looked on."

Benedick and Beatrice are engaged in a long standing feud: "You must, sir, mistake my niece; there is a kind of merry war betwixt Signior Benedick and her; they never meet but there is a skirmish of wit between them."

c. Don Pedro offers to woo Hero in Claudio's name and win her hand for him: "I will assume thy part in some disguise, and tell fair Hero I am Claudio; And in her bosom I'll unclasp my heart and take her hearing prisoner with the force and strong encounter of my amorous tale. Then, after, to her father will I break; and the conclusion is, she shall be thine."

4.
d. Answers will vary, but the following is a sample.

A messenger has brought a letter to Leonato, governor of Messina, informing him that Don Pedro, Prince of Arragon, and his men are coming to Messina, having been away fighting in a war. All are happy of the news, but Leonato's niece, Beatrice, asks if Benedick, a lord of Padua, is with the troop. She has been involved in a long-standing feud with him and takes every opportunity to jest about him...

d. Discuss with your teacher what you have read. On a separate piece of paper, write a narration of what has taken place. A **narration** is simply a retelling of the scene in your own words. You will be adding to this as you read the play so keep your narration papers together.

Throughout this unit will be suggested passages for you to read aloud with your teacher. Keep in mind what you have learned about the passage by having read the entire scene, worked the exercises, and written your narration. This should give you a thorough understanding of the scene, so read with expression. Here is your first scene taken from Act I, Scene I.

(Excerpt from the play, Act I, Scene I)

Claudio.   Benedick, didst thou note the daughter of Signior Leonato?

Benedick.   I noted her not, but I looked on her.

Claudio.   Is she not a modest young lady?

Benedick.   Do you question me as an honest man should do, for my simple true judgment? Or would you have me speak after my custom, as being a professed tyrant to their sex?

Claudio.   No, I pray thee speak in sober judgment.

Benedick.   Why, I' faith, methinks she's too low for a high praise, too brown for a fair praise, and too little for a great praise. Only this commendation I can afford her, that were she other than she is, she were unhandsome, and being no other but as she is, I do not like her.

Claudio.   Thou thinkest I am in sport. I pray thee tell me truly how thou lik'st her.

Benedick.   Would you buy her, that you inquire after her?

Claudio.   Can the world buy such a jewel?

Benedick.   Yea, and a case to put it into. But speak you this with a sad brow? Or do you play the flouting Jack, to tell us Cupid is a good hare-finder and Vulcan a rare carpenter? Come, in what key shall a man take you to go in the song?

Claudio.   In mine eye she is the sweetest lady that ever I looked on.

Benedick.   I can see yet without spectacles, and I see no such matter. There's her cousin, and she were not possessed with a fury, exceeds her as much in beauty as the first of May doth the last of December. But I hope you have no intent to turn husband, have you?

Claudio.   I would scarce trust myself, though I had sworn the contrary, if Hero would be my wife.

Benedick.   Is't come to this? In faith, hath not the world one man but he will wear his cap with suspicion? Shall I never see a bachelor of threescore again? Go to, in faith! And thou wilt needs thrust thy neck into a yoke, wear the print of it and sigh away Sundays. Look! Don Pedro is returned to seek you.

5. a. Read your narration from yesterday.

   b. Read Act I, Scene II and III aloud.

   c. In Scene III we are introduced to the villain of the piece. Who is he?

   d. He speaks of his *cage*. What is he referring to?

   e. Write your narration of these two scenes on a separate sheet of paper.

   f. Edit this week's narration up to this point. Check spelling and punctuation, and make a neat copy on the pages provided at the end of Lesson 32 in your *Student Activity Book*. OR you may complete this on a separate piece of paper.

5.
c. Don John

d. Don John has only recently been accepted back into his brother's good graces. He feels "caged" in that he is having to behave himself.

1.
a. Answers will vary.

c. The misunderstanding is resolved with Don Pedro's speech:
"Here, Claudio, I have wooed in thy name, and fair Hero is won. I have broke with her father, and his good-will obtained. Name the day of marriage, and God give thee joy!"

d. Don Pedro proposes to make Beatrice and Benedick fall in love with each other:
"...to bring Signior Benedick and the Lady Beatrice into a mountain of affection the one with the other. I would fain have it a match; and I doubt not but to fashion it if you three will but minister such assistance as I shall give you direction."

Claudio and Leonato agree to help him in this scheme.

e. Answers will vary.

1. a. Review what has taken place thus far. What mischief do you think Don John plans? Why?

   b. Read Act II, Scene I. The conversations after the revelers enter can be a bit confusing. Remember, everyone is wearing a mask, but most know who the other is. Also, pair off the speakers. While on stage together, they are having private conversations:

   > Don Pedro and Hero
   > Balthazar and Margaret
   > Ursula and Antonio
   > Benedick and Beatrice

   c. Don John knows very well he is speaking to Claudio. After their conversation, Claudio feels that Don Pedro has betrayed him. Is this misunderstanding resolved?

   d. What deed does Don Pedro, Claudio, and Leonato plan to accomplish before Claudio's and Hero's wedding?

   e. After reading the exchanges between Beatrice and Benedick, do you think their plan will succeed?

   f. Write your narration of this scene.

   g. Read the following scene aloud.

   (Excerpt from the play, Act II, Scene I)

   Leonato.   Count, take of me my daughter, and with her my fortunes. His Grace hath made the match, and all grace say amen to it!

   Beatrice.   Speak, count, 'tis your cue.

   Claudio.   Silence is the perfectest herald of joy. I were but little happy if I could say how much. Lady, as you are mine, I am yours. I give away myself for you and dote upon the exchange.

   Beatrice.   Speak, cousin; or (if you cannot) stop his mouth with a kiss and let not him speak neither.

Don Pedro.   In faith, lady, you have a merry heart.

Beatrice.   Yea, my lord; I thank it, poor fool, it keeps on the windy side of care. My cousin tells him in his ear that he is in her heart.

Claudio.   And so she doth, cousin.

Beatrice.   Thus goes everyone to the world but I, and I am sunburnt. I may sit in a corner and cry "Heigh-ho for a husband!"

Don Pedro. Lady Beatrice, I will get you one.

Beatrice.   I would rather have one of your father's getting. Hath your Grace ne'er a brother like you? Your father got excellent husbands, if a maid could come by them.

Don Pedro. Will you have me, lady?

Beatrice.   No, my lord, unless I might have another for working days; your Grace is too costly to wear every day. But I beseech your Grace pardon me. I was born to speak all mirth and no matter.

Don Pedro. Your silence most offends me, and to be merry best becomes you, for out o' question you were born in a merry hour.

Beatrice.   No, sure, my lord, my mother cried; but then there was a star danced, and under that was I born. Cousins, God give you joy!

Leonato.   Niece, will you look to those things I told you of?

Beatrice.   I cry you mercy, uncle. By your Grace's pardon.
Exit Beatrice.

Don Pedro. By my troth, a pleasant-spirited lady.

Leonato.   There's litte of the melancholy element in her, my lord. She is never sad but when she sleeps, and not ever sad then; for I have heard my daughter say she hath often dreamt of unhappiness and waked herself with laughing.

Don Pedro. She cannot endure to hear tell of a husband.

Leonato.   O, by no means! She mocks all her wooers out of suit.

Don Pedro. She were an excellent wife for Benedick.

2. a. Read Act II, Scene II. The wicked Don John is at it again. Add his evil plan to your narration.

   b. Act II, Scene III is one of the funniest scenes in the play as Benedick hides in the arbor and listens to a conversation meant for his ears. Read the scene.

2.

c. Benedick thinks that falling in love makes one act a fool. He does not believe it could happen to him:
" May I be so converted, and see with these eyes? I cannot tell: I think not."

At the end of the scene Benedick is convinced of Beatrice's love and is moved to return it. About this change he says:
"...I have railed so long against marriage; but doth not the appetite alter?" and...
"When I said I would die a bachelor I did not think I should live till I were married."

   c. Compare Benedick's thoughts about his marrying at the beginning of the scene to those expressed at the end of the scene. Why do you think they change?

   d. Read the following excerpt taken from the play, Act II, Scene III with your teacher:

Don Pedro. Come hither, Leonato. What was it you told me of today? That your niece Beatrice was in love with Signior Benedick?

Claudio.   O ay! [In a low voice to Don Pedro] Stalk on, stalk on; the fowl sits. [In full voice] I did never think that lady would have loved any man.

Leonato.   No, nor I neither; but most wonderful that she should so dote on Signior Benedick, whom she hath in all outward behaviors seemed ever to abhor.

Benedick.   [Aside] Is't possible? Sits the wind in that corner?

Leonato.   By my troth, my lord, I cannot tell what to think of it, but that she loves him with an enraged affection, it is past the infinite of thought.

Don Pedro. May be she doth but counterfeit.

Claudio. Faith, like enough.

Leonato. Counterfeit? There was never counterfeit of passion came so near the life of passion as she discovers it.

Don Pedro. Why, what affects of passion shows she?

Claudio. [In a low voice] Bait the hook well! This fish will bite.

Leonato. What affects, my lord? She will sit you, you heard my daughter tell you how.

Claudio. She did indeed.

Don Pedro. How, how, I pray you? You amaze me! I would have thought her spirit had been invincible against all assaults of affection.

Leonato. I would have sworn it had, my lord - especially against Benedick.

Benedick. [Aside] I should think this a gull but that the white-bearded fellow speaks it. Knavery cannot, sure, hide himself in such reverence.

Claudio. [In a low voice] He hat ta'en th' infection; hold it up.

Don Pedro. Hath she made her affection known to Benedick?

Leonato. No, and swears she never will. That's her torment.

Claudio. 'Tis true indeed. So your daughter says. "Shall I," says she, "that have so oft encount'red him with scorn, write to him that I love him?

Leonato. This says she now when she is beginning to write to him; for she'll be up twenty times a night and there will she sit in her smock till she have writ a sheet of paper. My daughter tells us all.

Leonato. O she tore the letter into a thousand half pence, railed at herself that she should be so immodest to write to one that she knew would flout her. "I measure him," says she, "by my own spirit; for I should flout him if he writ to me. Yea, though I love him, I should."

Claudio. Then down upon her knees she falls, weeps, sobs, beats her heart, tears her hair, prays, curses - "O sweet Benedick! God give me patience!"

Leonato. She doth indeed; my daughter says so; and the ecstacy hath so much overborne her that my daughter is sometime afeard she will do a desperate outrage to herself. It is very true.

Don Pedro. It were good that Benedick knew of it by some other, if she will not discover it.

Claudio. To what end! He would make but a sport of it and torment the poor lady worse.

Don Pedro. And he should, it were an alms to hand him! She's an excellent sweet lady, and out of all suspicion, she is virtuous.

Claudio. And she is exceeding wise.

Don Pedro. In everything but in loving Benedick.

3.
a. yes

b. Yes, the mood changes from a light comedy and becomes very serious. "O day untowardly turned."

c. Answers will vary.

3. a. It is now Beatrice's turn to have "the false sweet bait" dangled before her. Read Act III, Scene I. Does she take the bait?

b. Read Act III, Scene II aloud. The **mood** is how the writing makes you feel, such as happy, sad, peaceful, fearful, etc. Is there a mood change?

c. Will Don John's evil plan succeed?

d. Write your narration of these two scenes.

e. Read the following scene aloud.

(Excerpt from the play, Act III, Scene II)

Don John.   My lord and brother, God save you.

Don Pedro.   Good den, brother.

Don John.   If your leisure served, I would speak with you.

Don Pedro.   In private?

Don John.   If it pleases you. Yet Count Claudio may hear, for what I would speak of concerns him.

Don Pedro.   What's the matter?

Don John.   [To Claudio] Means your lordship to be married tomorrow?

Don Pedro.   You know he does.

Don John.   I know not that, when he knows what I know.

Claudio.   If there be any impediment, I pray you discover it.

Don John.   You may think I love you not; let that appear hereafter, and aim better at me but that I now will manifest. For my brother (I think he holds you well, and in dearness of heart) hath help to effect your ensuing marriage - surely suit ill spent and labor ill bestowed!

Don Pedro.   Why, what's the matter?

Don John.   I came hither to tell you, and, circumstances short'ned (for she has been too long a-talking of), the lady is disloyal.

Claudio.   Who? Hero?

Don John.   Even she - Leonato's Hero, your Hero, every man's Hero.

Claudio.   Disloyal?

Don John. The word is too good to paint out her wickedness. I could say she were worse. Think you of a worse title, and I will fit her to it. Wonder not till further warrant. Go but with me tonight, you shall see her chamber window ent'red even the night before her wedding day. If you love her then, tomorrow wed her. But it would better fit your honor to change your mind.

Claudio. May this be so?

Don Pedro. I will not think it.

Don John. If you dare not trust that you see, confess not that you know. If you will follow me, I will show you enough; and when you have seen more and heard more, proceed accordingly.

Claudio. If I see anything tonight why I should not marry her tomorrow, in the congregation where I should wed, there will I shame her.

Don John. I will disparage her no further till you are my witnesses. Bear it coldly but till midnight and let the issue show itself.

Don Pedro. O day untowardly turned!

Claudio. O mischief strangely thwarting!

Don John. O plague right well prevented! So will you say when you have seen the sequel.

4. a. In the next scene we are introduced to two very comic fellows - Dogberry and Verges, the local peace officers, who speak much nonsense. Read Act III, Scene III. What does Borachio brag about to Conrade?

   b. Write your narration of this scene on a separate piece of paper.

   c. Read Act III, Scene IV and write your narration of this scene on a separate piece of paper.

   d. Read the following scene aloud.

4.
a. Borachio boasts of his part in tricking Claudio and the prince into thinking Hero has been unfaithful to Claudio.

(Excerpt from the play, Act III, Scene III)

Dogberry.   Are you good men and true?

Verges.   Yea, or else it were pity but they should suffer salvation, body and soul.

Dogberry.   Nay, that were a punishment too good for them if they should have any allegiance in them, being chosen for the Prince's watch.

Verges.   Well, give them their charge, neighbor Dogberry.

Dogberry.   First,who think you the most desartless man to be constable?

First Watch. Hugh Oatcake, sir, or George Seacole, for they can write and read.

Dogberry.   Come hither, neighbor Seacole. God hath blessed you with a good name. To be a well-favored man is the gift of fortune, but to write and read comes by nature.

Second Watch. Both which, Master Constable -

Dogberry.   You have; I knew it would be your answer. Well, for your favor, sir, why, give God thanks and make no boast of it; and for your writing and reading, let that appear when there is no need of such vanity. You are thought here to be the most senseless and fit man for the constable of the watch. Therefore bear you the lanthorn. This is your charge: you shall comprehend all vagrom men; you are to bid any man stand, in the Prince's name.

Second Watch. How if 'a will not stand?

Dogberry.   Why then, take no note of him, but let him go, and presently call the rest of the watch together and thank God you are rid of a knave.

Verges.   If he will not stand when he is bidden, he is none of the Prince's subjects.

Dogberry.   True, and they are to meddle with none but the Prince's subjects. You shall also make no noise in the streets; for, for the watch to babble and to talk is most tolerable, and not to be endured.

Watch.   We will rather sleep than talk; we know what belongs to a watch.

Dogberry.   Why, you speak like an ancient and most quiet watchman, for I cannot see how sleeping should offend. Only, have a care that your bills be not stol'n. Well, you are to call at all the alehouses and bid those that are drunk get them to bed.

Watch.   How if they will not?

Dogberry.   Why then, let them alone till they are sober. If they make you not then the better answer, you may say they are not the men you took them for.

Watch.   Well, sir.

Dogberry.   If you meet a thief, you may suspect him by virtue of your office, to be no true man; and for such kind of men, the less you meddle or make with them, why, the more is for your honesty.

Watch.   If we know him to be a thief, shall we not lay hands on him?

Dogberry.   Truly, by your office you may; but I think they that touch pitch will be defiled. The most peaceable way for you, if you do take a thief, is to let him show himself what he is, and steal out of your company.

Verges.   You have been always called a merciful man, partner.

Dogberry.   Truly, I would not hang a dog by my will, much more a man who hath any honesty in him.

Verges.   If you hear a child cry in the night, you must call to the nurse and bid her still it.

Watch.   How if the nurse be asleep and will not hear us?

Dogberry.   Why then, depart in peace and let the child wake her
                with crying; for the ewe that will not hear her lamb
                when it bases will never answer a calf when he bleats.

Verges.   'Tis very true.

5. a. In this humorous scene with the two silly officers, Leonato
        is, unfortunately, in too much of a hurry to listen to their tale.
        Read Act III, Scene V. Dogberry wants the writer to take
        down their "excommunication." Do you think this is the
        word he meant to use?

    b. Write your narration of this scene on a separate piece of
        paper.

    c. The scene has been set for the exciting conclusion to the play
        which we will read next week. Today go back over this
        week's narration. Correct any punctuation or spelling errors
        and edit it. Make a neat copy in your *Student Activity Book*,
        or you may use a separate piece of paper.

5.
a. No.
He meant to record their communication or testimony.

1.

b. Beatrice entreats Benedick to challenge Claudio to a duel. He finally agrees.
"Enough, I am engaged. I will challenge him. I will kiss your hand and so leave you. By this hand, Claudio shall render me a dear account."

l. a. Read Act IV, Scene I. This is the climax of the play. The **climax** is usually the most intense part of the play. It is the high point or turning point of the plot.

b. Discuss the friar's plan. What does Beatrice ask Benedick to do? Why? Does he agree?

c. Write your narration of this emotional scene.

d. Read the following scene aloud, with feeling.

(Excerpt from the play Act IV, Scene I)

Benedick.   Lady Beatrice, have you wept all this while?

Beatrice.   Yea, and I will weep a while longer.

Benedick.   I will not desire that.

Beatrice.   You have no reason. I do it freely.

Benedick.   Surely I do believe your fair cousin is wronged.

Beatrice.   Ah, how much might the man deserve of me that would right her!

Benedick.   Is there any way to show such friendship?

Beatrice.   A very even way, but no such friend.

Benedick.   May a man do it?

Beatrice.   It is a man's office, but not yours.

Benedick.   I do love nothing in the world so well as you. Is not that strange?

Beatrice.   As strange as the think I know not. It were as possible for me to say I loved nothing so well as you. But believe me not; and yet I lie not. I confess nothing, nor I deny nothing. I am sorry for my cousin.

Benedick.   By my sword, Beatrice, thou lovest me.

Beatrice.   Do not swear and eat it.

Benedick.   I will swear by it that you love me, and I will make him eat it that says I love not you.

Beatrice.   Will you not eat your word?

Benedick.   With no sauce that can be devised to it. I protest I love thee.

Beatrice.   Why then, God forgive me!

Benedick.   What offense, sweet Beatrice?

Beatrice.   You have stayed me in a happy hour. I was about to protest I loved you.

Benedick.   And do it with all your heart.

Beatrice.   I love you with so much of my heart that none is left to protest.

Benedick.   Come, bid me do anything for thee.

Beatrice.   Kill Claudio.

Benedick.   Ha! Not for the wide world!

Beatrice.   You kill me to deny it. Farewell.

Benedick.   Tarry, sweet Beatrice. [He holds her.]

Beatrice.   I am gone, though I am here; there is no love in you. Nay, I pray you let me go!

Benedick.   Beatrice—

Beatrice.   In faith, I will go!

Benedick.   We'll be friends first. [He lets her go.]

Beatrice.	You dare easier to be friends with me than fight with mine enemy.
Benedick.	Is Claudio thine enemy?
Beatrice.	Is 'a not approved in the height a villain, that hath slandered, scorned, dishonored my kinswoman? O that I were a man! What, bear her in hand until they come to take hands; and then, with public accusation, uncovered slander, unmitigated rancor - O God, that I were a man! I would eat his heart in the market place!
Benedick.	Hear me, Beatrice—
Beatrice.	Sweet Hero, she is wronged, she is sland'red, she is undone.
Benedick.	Beat—
Beatrice.	Princes and counties! Surely, a princely testimony, a goodly count, Cound Comfect; a sweet gallant surely! O that I were a man for his sake! Or that I had any friend would be a man for my sake! But manhood is melted into cursies, valor into compliment, and men are only turned into tongue, and trim ones too. He is now as valiant as Hercules that only tells a lie, and swears it. I cannot be a man with wishing; therefore I will die a woman with grieving.
Benedick.	Tarry, good Beatrice. By this hand, I love thee.
Beatrice.	Use if for my love some other way than swearing by it.
Benedick.	Think you in your soul the Count Claudio hath wronged Hero?
Beatrice.	Yea, as sure as I have a thought or a soul.
Benedick.	Enough, I am engaged. I will challenge him. I will kiss your hand, and so leave you. By this hand, Claudio shall render me a dear account. As you hear of me, so think of me. Go comfort your cousin. I must say she is dead. And so farewell.

2. a. Look up a definition of *slander*. Has Hero been slandered?

   b. Read Act IV, Scene II. Dogberry is again having trouble choosing the right word. He says "O villain! Thou wilt be condemned into everlasting redemption for this." Do you think he means "redemption?"

   c. This kind of mistake is called a malapropism. A **malapropism** is an unintentional pun (word or words used to suggest more than one possible meaning) that happens when two similar words are confused in the speaker's mind. The term comes from the name of a character, Mrs. Malaprop, in *The Rivals*, an English play from the late eighteenth century by Richard Brinsley Sheridan.

   d. Find another example of a malapropism in Dogberry's last speech in this scene.

   e. Write your narration of this scene on a separate piece of paper.

3. a. Read Act V, Scene I. Why does Claudio say "I have drunk poison whiles he uttered it?"

   b. What is Leonato's plan? Who is the niece he speaks of?

   c. Another witty encounter between Benedick and his lady Beatrice occurs in Act V, Scene II. Read this scene.

   d. Write your narration of these two scenes on a separate piece of paper.

   e. Read the following scene aloud.

   (Excerpt from the play, Act V, Scene I)

Don Pedro. How now? Two of my brother's men bound? Borachio one.

Claudio. Hearken after their offense, my lord.

Don Pedro. Officers, what offense have these men done?

2.
a. Slander is a malicious, false, and defamatory report. Hero has indeed been slandered.

b. No, he means perdition.

d. "Doesn't thou not suspect (respect) my years?"

3.
a. Claudio realizes the part he has played in ending the life of innocent Hero.

b. Leonato proposes that Claudio marry a "niece" of his (in reality, Hero) sight unseen.

Dogberry. Marry, sir, they have committed false report; moreover, they have spoken untruths; secondarily, they are slanders; sixth and lastly, they have belied a lady; thirdly, they have verified unjust things; and to conclude, they are lying knaves.

Don Pedro. First, I ask thee what they have done; thirdly, I ask thee what's their offense; sixth and lastly, why they are committed; and to conclude, what you lay to their charge.

Claudio. Rightly reasoned, and in his own division; and, by my troth, there's one meaning well suited.

Don Pedero. Who have you offended, masters, that you are thus bound to your answer? This learned constable is too cunning to be understood. What's your offense?

Borachio. Sweet Prince, let me go no farther to mine answer. Do you hear me, and let this count kill me. I have deceived even your very eyes. What your wisdoms could not discover, these shallow fools have brought to light, who in the night overheard me confessing to this man, how Don John your brother incensed me to slander the Lady Hero; how you were brought into the orchard and saw me court Margaret in Hero's garments; how you disgraced her when you should marry her. My villainy they have upon record, which I had rather seal with my death than repeat over to my shame. The lady is dead upon mine and my master's false accusation; and briefly, I desire nothing but the reward of a villain.

Don Pedro. Runs not this speech like iron through your blood?

Claudio. I have drunk poison whiles he uttered it.

Don Pedro. But did my brother set thee on to this?

Borachio. Yea, and paid me richly for the practice of it.

Don Pedro. He is composed and framed of treachery, and fled he is upon this villainy.

Claudio.   Sweet Hero, now thy image doth appear in the rare
                semblance that I loved it first.

Dogberry.   Come, bring away the plaintiffs. By this time our
                sexton hath reformed Signior Leonato of the matter.

4. a. As Claudio's first penance, he must hang an epitaph on Hero's
      tomb and publicly confess his guilt and her innocence. Read
      Act V, Scene III.

   b. Write your narration on a separate piece of paper.

   c. The day of the wedding brings a happy ending. Read Act V,
      Scene IV. When Benedick says "And I do with an eye of love
      requite her," why does Leonato reply, "The sight whereof, I
      think, you had from me, from Claudio, and the prince?"

   d. Write your narration of this scene of a separate piece of
      paper.

   e. Enjoy reading the closing scene aloud.

   (Excerpt from the play, Act V, Scene IV)

Claudio.   For this I owe you. Here comes other reck'nings.
                Which is the lady I must seize upon?

Antonio.   This same is she, and I do give you her.

Claudio.   Why then, she's mine. Sweet, let me see your face.

Leonato.   No, that you shall not till you take her hand before this
                friar and swear to marry her.

Claudio.   Give me your hand; before this holy friar I am your
                husband if you like of me.

Hero.   And when I lived I was your other wife; [unmasking]
                and when you loved you were my other husband.

Claudio.   Another Hero!

Hero.   Nothing certainer. One Hero died defiled; but I do live,
                and surely as I live, I am a maid.

4.
**c. Leonato is referring to
the Prince's scheme to
make Benedick think
Beatrice was in love with
him.**

Don Pedro. The former Hero! Hero that is dead!

Leonato. She died, my lord, but whiles her slander lived.

Friar. All this amazement can I quality. When, after that the holy rites are ended, I'll tell you largely of fair Hero's death. Meantime let wonder seem familiar, and to the chapel let us presently.

Benedick. Soft and fair, friar. Which is Beatrice?

Beatrice. [unmasking] I answer to that name. What is your will?

Benedick. Do you not love me?

Beatrice. Why, no; no more than reason.

Benedick. Why, then your uncle, and the Prince, and Claudio have been deceived - they swore you did.

Beatrice. Do not you love me?

Benedick. Troth, no; no more than reason.

Beatrice. Why, then my cousin, Margaret and Ursula are much deceived; for they did swear you did.

Benedick. They swore that you were almost sick for me.

Beatrice. They swore that you were well-nigh dead for me.

Benedick. 'Tis no such matter. Then you do not love me?

Beatrice. No, truly, but in friendly recompense.

Leonato. Come, cousin, I am sure you love the gentleman.

Claudio. And I'll be sworn upon't that he loves her; for here's a paper written in his hand. A halting sonnet of his own pure brain, fashioned to Beatrice.

Hero.   And here's another, writ in my cousin's hand, stol'n from her pocket, containing her affection unto Benedick.

Benedick.   A miracle! Here's our own hands against our hearts. Come, I will have thee; but, by this light, I take thee for pity.

Beatrice.   I would not deny you; but, by this good day, I yield upon great persuasion, and partly to save your life for I was told you were in a consumption.

Benedick.   Peace! I will stop your mouth. [kisses her]

Don Pedro.   How dost thou, Benedick, the married man?

Benedick.   I'll tell thee what, Prince: a college of witcrackers cannot flout me out of my humor. Dost thou think I care for a satire or an epigram? No. If a man will be beaten with brains, 'a shall wear nothing handsome about. In brief, since I do purpose to marry, I will think nothing to any purpose that the world can say against it; and therefore never flout at me for what I have said against it; for man is a giddy thing, and this is my conclusion.

5. a. Proofread and edit this week's narration. Make a final neat copy in your *Student Activity Book*, or you may use a separate piece of paper. You should now have a complete synopsis of *Much Ado About Nothing* similar to that from *Tales from Shakespeare*.

   b. Choose your favorite parts of the play and reread them aloud. If possible, act them out.

                              OR

   c. Optional: Read another play synopsis in *Tales from Shakespeare*.

Tales from Shakespeare

There lived in the palace at Messina two ladies, whose names were Hero and Beatrice. Hero was the daughter, and Beatrice the niece, of Leonato, the governor of Messina.

Beatrice was of a lively temper, and loved to divert her cousin Hero, who was of a more serious disposition, with her sprightly sallies. Whatever was going forward was sure to make matter of mirth for the light-hearted Beatrice.

At the time the history of these ladies commences some young men of high rank in the army, as they were passing through Messina on their return from a war that was just ended, in which they had distinguished themselves by their great bravery, came to visit Leonato. Among these were Don Pedro, the Prince of Arragon; and his friend Claudio, who was a lord of Florence; and with them came the wild and witty Benedick, and he was a lord of Padua.

These strangers had been at Messina before, and the hospitable governor introduced them to his daughter and his niece as their old friends and acquaintance.

Benedick, the moment he entered the room, began a lively conversation with Leonato and the prince. Beatrice, who liked not to be left out of any discourse, interrupted Bendick with saying, "I wonder that you will still be talking, signior Benedick: nobody marks you." Benedick was just such another rattle-brain as Beatrice, yet he was not pleased at this free salutation; he thought it did not become a well-bred lady to be so flippant with her tongue; and he remembered, when he was last at Messina, that Beatrice used to select him to make her merry jests upon. And as there is no one who so little likes to be made a jest of as those who are apt to take the same liberty themselves, so it was with Benedick and Beatrice; these two sharp wits never met in former times but a perfect war of raillery was kept up between them, and they always parted mutually displeased with each other. Therefore when Beatrice stopped him in the middle of his discourse, telling him nobody marked what he was saying, Benedick, affecting not to have observed before that she was present, said, "What, my dear lady Disdain, are you yet living?" And now war broke out afresh between them, and a long jangling argument ensued, during which Beatrice, although she knew he had so well approved his valour in the late war, said that she would eat all he had killed there: and observing the prince take delight in Benedick's conversation, she called him "the prince's jester." This sarcasm sunk deeper into the mind of Benedick than all Beatrice had said before. The hint she gave him that he was a coward, by saying she would eat all he had killed, he did not regard, knowing himself to be a brave man; but there is nothing that great wits so much dread as the imputation of buffoonery, because the charge comes sometimes a little too near the truth: therefore Benedick perfectly hated Beatrice when she called him "the prince's jester."

The modest lady Hero was silent before the noble guests; and while Claudio was attentively observing the improvement which time had made in her beauty, and was contemplating the exquisite graces of her fine figure (for she was an admirable young lady), the prince was highly amused with listening to the humorous dialogue between

Benedick and Beatrice; and he said in a whisper to Leonato, "This is a pleasant-spirited young lady. She were an excellent wife for Benedick." Leonato replied to this suggestion, "O my lord, my lord, if they were but a week married, they would talk themselves mad." But though Leonato thought they would make a discordant pair, the prince did not give up the idea of matching these two keen wits together.

When the prince returned with Claudio from the palace, he found that the marriage he had devised between Benedick and Beatrice was not the only one projected in that good company, for Claudio spoke in such terms of Hero, as made the prince guess at what was passing in his heart; and he liked it well, and he said to Claudio, "Do you affect Hero?" To this question Claudio replied, "O my lord, when I was last at Messina, I looked upon her with a soldier's eye, that liked, but had no leisure for loving; but now, in this happy time of peace, thoughts of war have left their places vacant in my mind, and in their room come thronging soft and delicate thoughts, all prompting me how fair young Hero is, reminding me that I liked her before I went to the wars." Claudio's confession of his love for Hero so wrought upon the prince, that he lost no time in soliciting the consent of Leonato to accept of Claudio for a son-in-law. Leonato agreed to this proposal, and the prince found no great difficulty in persuading the gentle Hero herself to listen to the suit of the noble Claudio, who was a lord of rare endowments, and highly accomplished, and Claudio, assisted by his kind prince, soon prevailed upon Leonato to fix an early day for the celebration of his marriage with Hero.

Claudio was to wait for a few days before he was to be married to his fair lady; yet he complained of the interval being tedious, as indeed most young men are impatient when they are waiting for the accomplishment of any event they have set their hearts upon: the prince, therefore, to make the time seem short to him, proposed as a kind of merry pastime that they should invent some artful scheme to make Benedick and Beatrice fall in love with each other. Claudio entered with great satisfaction into this whim of the prince, and Leonato promised them his assistance, and even Hero said she would do any modest office to help her cousin to a good husband.

The device the prince invented was, that the gentlemen should make Benedick believe that Beatrice was in love with him, and that Hero should make Beatrice believe that Benedick was in love with her.

The prince, Leonato, and Claudio began their operations first: and watching an opportunity when Benedick was quietly seated reading in an arbour, the prince and his assistants took their station among the trees behind the arbour, so near that Benedick could not choose but hear all they said; and after some careless talk the prince said, "Come hither, Leonato. What was it you told me the other day—that your niece Beatrice was in love with signior Benedick? I did never think that lady would have loved any man." "No, nor I neither, my lord," answered Leonato. "It is most wonderful that she should so dote on Benedick, whom she in all outward behaviour seemed ever to dislike." Claudio confirmed all this was saying that Hero had told him Beatrice was so in love with Benedick, that she would certainly die of grief, if he could not be brought to love her; which Leonato and Claudio seemed to agree was impossible, he having always been such a railer against all fair ladies, and in particular against Beatrice.

The prince affected to hearken to all this with great compassion for Beatrice, and he said, "It were good that Benedick were told of this." "To what end?" said Claudio; "he would but make sport of it, and torment the poor lady worse." "And if he should," said the prince, "it were a good deed to hang him; for Beatrice is an excellent sweet lady, and exceeding wise in everything but in loving Benedick." Then the prince motioned to his companions that they should walk on, and leave Benedick to meditate upon what he had overheard.

Benedick had been listening with great eagerness to this conversation; and he said to himself when he heard Beatrice loved him, "Is it possible? Sits the wind in that corner?" And when they were gone, he began to reason this manner with himself: "This can be no trick!" They were very serious, and they have the truth from Hero, and seem to pity the lady. Love me! Why it must be requited! I did never think to marry. But when I said I should die a bachelor, I did not think I should live to be married. They say the lady is virtuous and fair. She is so. And wise in everything but in loving me. Why, that is no great argument of her folly. But here comes Beatrice. By this day, she is a fair lady. I do spy some marks of love in her." Beatrice now approached him, and said with her usual tartness, "Against my will I am sent to bid you come in to dinner." Benedick, who never felt himself disposed to speak so politely to her before, replied, "Fair Beatrice, I thank you for your pains:" and when Beatrice, after two or three more rude speeches, left him, Benedick thought he observed a concealed meaning of kindness under the uncivil words she uttered, and he said aloud, "If I do not take pity on her, I am a villain. If I do not love her, I am a Jew. I will go get her picture."

The gentleman being thus caught in the net they had spread for him, it was now Hero's turn to play her part with Beatrice; and for this purpose she sent for Ursula and Margaret, two gentlewomen who attended upon her, and she said to Margaret, "Good Margaret, run to the parlour; there you will find my cousin Beatrice talking with the prince and Claudio. Whisper in her ear, that I and Ursula are walking in the orchard, and that our discourse is all of her. Bid her steal into that pleasant arbour, where honeysuckles, ripened by the sun, like ungrateful minions, forbid the sun to enter." This arbour, into which Hero desired Margaret to entice Beatrice, was the very same pleasant arbour where Benedick had so lately been an attentive listener.

"I will make her come, I warrant, presently," said Margaret.

Hero, then taking Ursula with her into the orchard, said to her, "Now Ursula, when Beatrice comes, we will walk up and down this alley, and our talk must be only of Benedick, and when I name him, let it be your part to praise him more than ever man did merit. My talk to you must be how Benedick is in love with Beatrice. Now begin; for look where Beatrice like a lapwing runs close by the ground, to hear our conference." They then began; Hero saying, as if in answer to something which Ursula had said, "No, truly, Ursula. She is too disdainful; her spirits are as coy as wild birds of the rock." "But are you sure," said Ursula, "that Benedick loves Beatrice so entirely?" Hero replied, "So says the prince, and my lord Claudio, and they entreated me to acquaint her with it; but I persuaded them, if they loved Benedick, never to let Beatrice know of it." "Certainly," replied Ursula, "it were not good she knew his love, lest she made sport of it." "Why, to say truth," said Hero, "I never yet saw a man, how wise soever, or noble, young, or rarely featured, but she would dispraise him." "Sure, sure, such carping is not commendable," said Ursula. "No," replied Hero, "but who dare tell her so? If I should speak, she would mock me into air." "O! you wrong your cousin," said Ursula: "she cannot be so much without true judgment, as to refuse so rare a gentleman as signior Benedick." "He hath an excellent good name," said Hero: "indeed, he is the first man in Italy, always excepting my dear Claudio." And now, Hero giving her attendant a hint that it was time to change the discourse, Ursula said, "And when are you to be married, madam?" Hero then told her, that she was to be married to Claudio the next day, and desired she would go in with her, and look at some new attire, as she wished to consult with her on what she would wear on the morrow. Beatrice, who had been listening with breathless eagerness to this dialogue, when they went away, exclaimed, "What fire is in mine ears? Can this be true? Farewell, contempt and scorn, and maiden pride, adieu! Benedick, love on! I will requite you, taming my wild heart to your loving hand."

It must have been a pleasant sight to see these old enemies converted into new and loving friends, and to behold their first meeting after being cheated into mutual liking by the merry artifice of the good-humoured prince. But a sad reverse in the fortunes of Hero must now be thought of. The morrow, which was to have been her wedding-day, brought sorrow on the heart of Hero and her good father Leonato.

The prince had a half-brother, who came from the wars along with him to Messina. This brother (his name was Don John) was a melancholy, discontented man, whose spirits seemed to labour in the contriving of villanies. He hated the prince his brother, and he hated Claudio, because he was the prince's friend, and determined to prevent Claudio's marriage with Hero, only for the malicious pleasure of making Claudio and the prince unhappy; for he knew the prince had set his heart upon this marriage, almost as much as Claudio himself; and to effect this wicked purpose, he employed one Borachio, a man as bad as himself, whom he encouraged with the offer of a great reward. This Borachio paid his court to Margaret, Hero's attendant; and Don John, knowing this, prevailed upon him to make Margaret promise to talk with him from her lady's chamber window that night, after Hero was asleep, and also to dress herself in Hero's clothes, the better to deceive Claudio into the belief that it was Hero; for that was the end he meant to compass by this wicked plot.

Don John then went to the prince and Claudio, and told them that Hero was an imprudent lady, and that she talked with men from her chamber-window at midnight. Now this was the evening before the wedding, and he offered to take them that night, where they should themselves hear Hero discoursing with a man from her window; and they consented to go along with him, and Claudio said, "If I see anything to-night why I should not marry her, to-morrow in the congregation, where I intended to wed her, there will I shame her.' The prince also said, "And as I assisted you to obtain her, I will join with you to disgrace her."

When Don John brought them near Hero's chamber that night, they saw Borachio standing under the window, and they saw Margaret looking out of Hero's window, and heard her talking with Borachio: and Margaret being dressed in the same clothes they had seen Hero wear, the prince and Claudio believed it was the lady Hero herself.

Nothing could equal the anger of Claudio, when he had made (as he thought) this discovery. All his love for the innocent Hero was at once converted into hatred, and he resolved to expose her in the church, as he had said he would, the next day; and the prince agreed to this, thinking no punishment could be too severe for the naughty lady, who talked with a man from her window the very night before she was going to be married to the noble Claudio.

The next day, when they were all met to celebrate the marriage, and Claudio and Hero were standing before the priest, and the priest, or friar, as he was called, was proceeding to pronounce the marriage ceremony, Claudio, in the most passionate language, proclaimed the guilt of the blameless Hero, who, amazed at the strange words he uttered, said meekly, "Is my lord well, that he does speak so wide?"

Leonato, in the utmost horror, said to the prince, "My lord, why speak not you?" "What should I speak?" said the prince; "I stand dishonoured, that have gone about to link my dear friend to an unworthy woman. Leonato, upon my honour, myself, my brother, and this grieved Claudio, did see and hear her last night at midnight talk with a man at her chamber window."

Benedick, in astonishment at what he heard, said, "This looks not like a nuptial."

"True, O God!" replied the heart-struck Hero; and then this hapless lady sunk down in a fainting fit, to all appearance dead. The prince and Claudio left the church, without staying to see if Hero would recover, or at all regarding the distress into which they had thrown Leonato. So hard-hearted had their anger made them.

Benedick remained, and assisted Beatrice to recover Hero from her swoon, saying, "How does the lady?" "Dead, I think," replied Beatrice in great agony, for she loved her cousin; and knowing her virtuous principles, she believed nothing of what she had heard spoken against her. Not so the poor old father; he believed the story of his child's shame, and it was piteous to hear him lamenting over her, as she lay like one dead before him, wishing she might never more open her eyes.

But the ancient friar was a wise man, and full of observation on human nature, and he had attentively marked the lady's countenance when she heard herself accused, and noted a thousand blushing shames to start into her face, and then he saw an angel-like whiteness bear away those blushes, and in her eye he saw a fire that did belie the error that the prince did speak against her maiden truth, and he said to the sorrowing father, "Call me a fool; trust not my reading, nor my observation; trust not my age, my reverence, nor my calling, if this sweet lady lie not guiltless here under some biting error."

When Hero had recovered from the swoon into which she had fallen, the friar said to her, "Lady, what man is he you are accused of?" Hero replied, "They know that do accuse me; I know of none:" then turning to Leonato, she said, "O my father, if you can prove that any man has ever conversed with me at hours unmeet, or that I yesternight changed words with any creature, refuse me, hate me, torture me to death."

"There is," said the friar, "some strange misunderstanding in the prince and Claudio;" and then he counselled Leonato, that he should report that Hero was dead; an he said that the death-like swoon in which they had left Hero would make this easy of belief; and he also advised him that he should put on mourning, and erect a monument for her, and do all rites that appertain to a burial. "What shall become of this?" said Leonato; "what will this do?" The friar replied, "This report of her death shall change slander into pity: that is some good; but that is not all the good I hope for. When Claudio shall hear she died upon hearing his words, the idea of her life shall sweetly creep into his imagination. Then shall he mourn, if ever love had interest in his heart, and wish that he had not so accused her; yea, though he thought his accusation true."

Benedick now said, "Leonato, let the friar advise you; and though you know how well I love the prince and Claudio, yet on my honour I will not reveal this secret to them."

Leonato, thus persuaded, yielded; and he said sorrowfully, "I am so grieved, that the smallest twine may lead me." The kind friar then led Leonato and Hero away to comfort and console them, and Beatrice and Benedick remained alone; and this was the meeting from which their friends, who contrived the merry plot against them, expected so much diversion; those friends who were now overwhelmed with affliction, and from whose minds all thoughts of merriment seemed for ever banished.

Benedick was the first who spoke, and he said, "Lady Beatrice, have you wept all this while?" "Yea, and I will weep a while longer," said Beatrice. "Surely," said Benedick, "I do believe your fair cousin is wronged." "Ah!" said Beatrice, "how much might that man deserve of me who would right her!" Benedick then said, "Is there any way to show such friendship? I do love nothing in the world so well as you: is not that strange?" "It were as possible," said Beatrice, "for me to say I loved nothing in the world so well as you; but believe me not, and yet I lie not. I confess nothing, nor I deny nothing. I am sorry for my cousin." "By my sword," said Benedick, "you love me, and I protest I love you. Come, bid me do anything for you." "Kill Claudio," said Beatrice. "Ha! not for the wide world," said Benedick; for he loved his friend Claudio, and he believed he had been imposed upon. "Is not Claudio a villain, that has slandered, scorned, and dishonoured my cousin?" said Beatrice: "O that I were a man!" "Hear me, Beatrice!" said Benedick. But Beatrice would hear nothing in Claudio's defence; and she continued to urge on Benedick to revenge her cousin's wrongs: and she said, "Talk with a man out of the window; a proper saying! Sweet Hero! she is wronged; she is slandered; she is undone. O that I were a man for Claudio's sake! or that I had any friend, who would be a man for my sake! but valour is melted into courtesies and compliments. I cannot be a man with wishing, therefore I will die a woman with grieving." "Tarry, good Beatrice," said Benedick: "by this hand I love you." "Use it for my love some other way than swearing by it," said Beatrice. "Think you on your soul, that Claudio has wronged Hero?" asked Benedick. "Yea," answered Beatrice; "as sure as I have a thought, or a soul." "Enough," said Benedick; "I am engaged; I will challenge him. I will kiss your hand, and so leave you. By this hand, Claudio shall render me a dear account! As you hear from me, so think of me. Go, comfort your cousin."

While Beatrice was thus powerfully pleading with Benedick, and working his gallant temper by the spirit of her angry words, to engage in the cause of Hero, and fight even with his dear friend Claudio, Leonato was challenging the prince and Claudio to answer with their swords the injury they had done his child, who, he affirmed, had died for grief. But they respected his age and his sorrow, and they said, "Nay, do not quarrel with us, good old man." And now came Benedick, and he also challenged Claudio to answer with his sword the injury he had done to Hero; and Claudio and the prince said to each other, "Beatrice has set him on to do this." Claudio nevertheless must have accepted this challenge of Benedick, had not the justice of Heaven at the moment brought to pass a better proof of the innocence of Hero than the uncertain fortune of a duel.

While the prince and Claudio were yet talking of the challenge of Benedick, a magistrate brought Borachio as a prisoner before the prince. Borachio had been overheard talking with one of his companions of the mischief he had been employed by Don John to do.

Borachio made a full confession to the prince in Claudio's hearing, that it was Margaret dressed in her lady's clothes that he had talked with from the window, whom they had mistaken for the lady Hero herself; and no doubt continued on the minds of Claudio and the prince of the innocence of Hero. If a suspicion had remained it must have been removed by the flight of Don John, who, finding his villanies were detected, fled from Messina to avoid the just anger of his brother.

The heart of Claudio was sorely grieved when he found he had falsely accused Hero, who, he thought, died upon hearing his cruel words; and the memory of his beloved Hero's image came over him, in the rare semblance that he loved it first; and the prince asking him if what he heard did not run like iron through his soul, he answered, that he felt as if he had taken poison while Borachio was speaking.

And the repentant Claudio implored forgiveness of the old man Leonato for the injury he had done his child; and promised, that whatever penance Leonato would lay upon him for his fault in believing the false accusation against his betrothed wife, for her dear sake he would endure it.

The penance Leonato enjoined him was, to marry the next morning a cousin of Hero's, who, he said, was now his heir, and in person very like Hero. Claudio, regarding the solemn promise he made to Leonato, said, he would marry this unknown lady, even though she were an Ethiop: but his heart was very sorrowful, and he passed that night in tears, and in remoseful grief, at the tomb which Leonato had erected for Hero.

When the morning came, the prince accompanied Claudio to the church, where the good friar, and Leonato and his niece, were already assembled, to celebrate a second nuptial; and Leonato presented to Claudio his promised bride; and she wore a mask, that Claudio might not discover her face. And Claudio said to the lady in the mask, "Give me your hand, before this holy friar; I am your husband, if you will marry me." "And when I lived I was your other wife," said this unknown lady; and, taking off her mask, she proved to be no niece (as was pretended), but Leonato's very daughter, the lady Hero herself. We may be sure that this proved a most agreeable surprise to Claudio, who thought her dead, so that he could scarcely for joy believe his eyes; and the prince, who was equally amazed at what he saw, exclaimed, "Is not this Hero, Hero that was dead?" Leonato replied, "She died, my lord, but while her slander lived." The friar promised them an explanation of this seeming miracle, after the ceremony was ended; and was proceeding to marry them, when he was interrupted by Benedick, who desired to be married at the same time to Beatrice. Beatrice making some demur to this match, and Benedick challenging her with her love for him, which he had learned from Hero, a pleasant explanation took place; and they found they had both been tricked into a belief of love, which had never existed, and had become lovers in truth by the power of a false jest: but the affection, which a merry invention had cheated them into, was grown too powerful to be shaken by a serious explanation; and since Benedick proposed to marry, he was resolved to think nothing to the purpose that the world could say against it; and he merrily kept up the jest, and swore to Beatrice, that he took her but for pity, and because he heard she was dying of love for him; and Beatrice protested, that she yielded but upon great persuasion, and partly to save his life, for she heard he was in a consumption. So these two mad wits were reconciled, and made a match of it, after Claudio and Hero were married; and to complete the history, Don John, the contriver of the villany, was taken in his flight, and brought back to Messina; and a brave punishment it was to this gloomy, discontented man, to see the joy and feastings which, by the disappointment of his plots, took place at the palace in Messina.

The
Research Unit

The Research Unit is a four-week unit.

Prewriting

1. Choose a Topic

   a. The first important step in writing a research paper is choosing a topic. Your teacher may assign a specific topic or simply suggest a general topic, leaving it up to you to find a specific topic. In that case, choose a subject that you would like to know more about.

   b. It is important to limit your topic because it is difficult to handle research if your topic is too broad. Be sure to choose a subject that you are sure to find enough information about in order to write a good paper.

   > Ex: General area of interest: Science
   >   General topic: Insects
   >   Limited topic: Bees

2. Gather Sources

   a. After you have decided on a topic, spend some time in the library gathering sources of information.

   b. Begin by looking up information about your general topic in the library's card catalog, periodicals, and major encyclopedias.

   c. Do not rely on just one or two sources. Try to find as many varied sources as you can. If you cannot find what you need, ask the librarian to help you.

3. Bibliography

   a. Today, become acquainted with your sources.

   b. After scanning the books or articles you have checked out, you may find that some will not be useful to you.

   c. Now, compile a bibliography from the sources you have chosen. If you keep track of your sources during the research process, it will make writing the final bibliography much easier. These entries may be recorded on index cards.

Include the following facts:

1) Author (or editor)
2) Title (of book or article)
3) Publication facts
   - books: city, publisher, date
   - encyclopedias: name, year
   - periodicals: title, date, pages

d. You may also wish to include the library call number in case you need to find the source again.

The general format for a book reference is:

Author's name (last name first). <u>Title</u> (underlined). place of publication: publisher's name in full, copyright date.

The general format for a periodical (magazine) is:

Author's name (last name first). "Title of Article" (in quotation marks). <u>Name of Magazine</u> (underlined) date of publication: page reference.

Here is how to list articles in reference works:

Author's name (last name first). "Title of Article" (in quotation marks). <u>Name of the Encyclopedia.</u> date.

Ex:

Bibliography

Round, Buzz N. "All You Ever Wanted to Know About Honeybees." <u>The Beekeepers Magazine</u> May, 1992: pp. 23-27.

Sting, Nass T. "Bees." <u>The World Book Encyclopedia.</u> 1990 ed.

Sweet, I. M. <u>The Honey Book.</u> New York: MacMillan, 1935.

---

4. Prepare Note Cards and Take Notes

a. Before you begin your research, write down questions you would like to answer about your topic.

b. Ask the investigative questions:
Who?
What?
When?
Where?
Why?
How?

c. Put each question on a 3 x 5 card. You may use a case to keep them in. As you read, you will find information that answers your questions.

d. Write the information on another card and file it behind the appropriate question card. This will help you organize your paper later on.

The following are sample questions you might ask about bees:

- What do bees look like?
- What are the different kinds of bees?
- Where do bees live?
- Why do people keep bees?
- What are some unusual facts about bees?

e. Put information from <u>one</u> book or article on a notecard, indicating the author and title on the back of the card. You may need this to recheck information at a later date. Summarize the information in your own words.

f. If you must copy something, put quotation marks around it and indicate the source and page number where the quotation can be found. You may need to refer to it later.

g. It is best to write a single piece of information on each card. This will make it easier for you to arrange the cards in the order that best suits your paper.

5. Continue Taking Notes

   a. Refer to the checklist below to help you keep track of your progress.

   Student Checklist

   Week One - Prewriting   ❑
   Choose a Topic
   Gather Sources
   Bibliography
   Prepare Note Cards and Take Notes

   Week Two - Writing the First Draft ❑
   Working Outline
   Final Outline
   Write First Draft

   Week Three - Revising   ❑
   Revision One - Content
   Revision Two - Style

   Week Four - The Final Draft   ❑
   First Proofread
   Type or Write in Ink
   Final Proofread

   ---

   b. Because writing is a personal activity, it is difficult to make daily assignments. Everyone works at his or her own pace. The next three weeks' assignments are designed to help you pace yourself. Refer to this checklist to help you keep track of your progress.

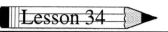

Writing the First Draft

1 & 2. Working Outline

  a. It would be helpful now to formulate a working outline. Look at the questions you wrote to help organize your notes. The information you have gathered will probably suggest a focus for your paper.

  b. For instance, after researching bees, you will find that most of the information you came across was about honeybees and their usefulness to man.

  c. Arrange your information in a logical order to make an outline.

  d. Using this order, write a list of your questions leaving some space between each question to record the main facts or examples from your note cards. Using the questions about bees, your working outline could look like this:

Why do people keep bees?
    honey for human consumption
    beeswax to make various products
    pollination of crops
    source of study

Where do bees live?
    beehive
    honeycomb

What do bees eat?
    nectar
    honey

What are some unusual facts about bees?
    highly developed society
    ability to distinguish taste
    ability to communicate

  e. This is a rough draft of the outline of your paper. Do you have enough information for each question? Is the information organized in a clear and logical order?

f. Take a little more time if necessary to finish gathering information. As you read through your questions and supporting information, you may find you need to collect more data or revise your topic.

3 & 4. Final Outline

Now you are ready to revise your outline into its final form. Rewrite your questions and main facts into sentence form. The questions will be the topics or main ideas and should be numbered in Roman numerals (I, II, III, etc.). The main facts under each question should be labeled with capital letters (A, B, C, etc.). If there is only one subpoint or only one example, there is no need to begin a new section.

Outline Guide

```
 I.  Topic

     A. Subpoint
     B. Subpoint
     C. Subpoint
     D. Subpoint

 II. Topic

     A. Subpoint
     B. Subpoint
     C. Subpoint

III. Topic

     A. Subpoint
     B. Subpoint
     C. Subpoint

IV. Topic

     A. Subpoint
     B. Subpoint
     C. Subpoint
```

Sample Sentence Outline

I. From the beginning, man has enjoyed many uses of bees.

    A. Honey is used to make bread, crackers, cookies, and other baked goods, as well as a sweet spread.

    B. Beeswax is used to make candles, lipstick, polishes and other products.

    C. Bees aid farmers by pollinating crops.

    D. Some people keep bees just to study their interesting habits.

II. Honeybees build their nests, called hives, out of beeswax shaping it into a honeycomb.

    A. The honeycomb is waterproof.

    B. The honeycomb is a mass of six-sided compartments or cells.

    C. The workers enlarge the hive by making more cells when needed to store the queen's eggs, pollen, or nectar.

III. Bees eat honey that they produce.

    A. Bees suck nectar from flowers with their long tongues, storing it in a honey stomach where it is mixed with chemicals.

    B. After returning to the hive, the bee sucks the nectar back into his stomach and puts it in an empty cell.

    C. As the water in the nectar evaporates, a chemical change takes place, turning the nectar into honey.

IV. People enjoy studying bees because of their interesting and unusual behavior.

    A. Bees live in a highly developed societal structure.

    B. Honeybees can identify if a flower has a sweet, sour, salty, or bitter taste.

    C. Bees are able to communicate to other bees in the hive the location of a distant nectar by dancing a certain pattern.

5. First Draft

   a. **Introductory Paragraph**
      You are ready to begin writing the first draft of your paper. Begin by writing an introductory paragraph. This will introduce your topic and should capture the attention of your readers. To do this, you might include a quote, a brief anecdote, a question, or a striking fact.

      Example:
      Of all the thousands of species of insects on the earth, only one produces food that can be eaten by man. The honeybee is one of God's most fascinating creations. Measuring a scant .5 inches with a life expectancy of only thirty-eight days, the amazing honeybee provides many services for mankind. Not the least of which is the delicious honey you spread on your toast each morning.

   b. **Middle Paragraphs**
      Next, write the middle paragraphs of your paper using your outline. The main ideas will be the topic sentences for each paragraph and the supporting sentences will supply the details. Cover each of the subpoints of the outline using transitional words such as *however, also, then, next* to connect the paragraphs.

      Example:
      From the beginning man has enjoyed many uses of bees. Honey has been used by bakers to make bread, crackers, cookies and other baked goods, as well as being used as a sweet spread. In addition, beeswax produced by honeybees is used to make candles, lipstick, polishes and other products. Honeybees also aid farmers by helping to pollinate their crops. Finally, some people keep honeybees just to study their interesting habits.

      Honeybees build their nests, called <u>hives</u>, out of beeswax, which they produce. They shape the hive into a honeycomb, a waterproof mass of six-sided compartments or cells....

c. **Concluding Paragraphs**

Finally, you need to write a concluding paragraph summing up the main ideas of your paper. Again, you might choose to use a quote or an anecdote to sum up the thrust of the paper.

Example:

In ancient times, a jar of honey on the table was a mark of great wealth. Today, we know that along with its good taste, it is also nutritionally good for you. Perhaps that is why King Solomon in his wisdom recommended honey in Proverbs 24:13, "My son, eat thou honey, because it is good; and the honeycomb, which is sweet to thy taste." The next time you place a honey jar on your table, consider the amazing work of the honeybee. Maybe the ancients were right after all.

Revising

Refer to the checklist in Lesson 33 to help you keep track of your progress. This week, you will be revising what you wrote last week. You will be directed to write two revisions. It is easier to concentrate on each of these areas of revision separately. When you finish the first revision, take a break. Start the second revision the third day.

1 & 2. Revision One - Content

   a. The first revision will have to do with <u>what</u> you wrote.

       1) Is there a paragraph for each subpoint of my outline?
       2) Does the information in each paragraph support its topic sentence?
       3) Is the information clear and concise?
       4) Did I say what I wanted to say?

   b. Next, read through your paper once again. This time you will be refining the style of your writing.

3 & 4. Revision Two - Style

   a. The second revision will have to do with <u>how</u> you wrote it.

       1) Is the sentence and paragraph structure correct?
       2) Do the sentences flow together smoothly?
       3) Have I chosen clear, strong nouns and verbs?
       4) Are there any short sentences that can be combined into more complex sentences?
       5) Am I too wordy?
       6) Is the sentence and paragraph structure correct?

5. a. Rewrite your paper to make any necessary changes.

    b. Finally, you may add one or more visual aids to enhance your report and make it more interesting. These could include such items as graphs, charts, or illustrations.

The Final Draft

1. First Proofread

   a. Refer to the checklist in Lesson 33 to help you keep track of your progress. To prepare for your final draft, read through your paper once more. This time look for any spelling, capitalization, punctuation, or grammar errors.

   b. Ask your teacher to proofread the paper for you.

2 & 3. Type or Write in Ink

   a. When everything has been corrected it is time to make a final copy. If possible, you should type the paper. If you cannot, make a neat final copy in ink.

   b. Your paper should include a Title Page containing the title of your paper, your name, and the date. The Bibliography should come after the body of the paper. Arrange the items alphabetically by author. Do not indent the first line of the bibliography entry, but do indent the following lines. See the sample bibliography in Lesson 33.

4 & 5. Final Proofread

   When you have finished, carefully proofread your paper looking for any typing or copying errors that may need to be corrected. After all corrections have been made, place your paper neatly in a cover.

Sample Title Page

> The Useful Honeybee *(Title of Paper)*
>
> Goodstudent *(Name of Student)*
>
> Mrs. Best Teacher *(Teacher's Name)*
>
> Language Arts 7 *(Course Name)*
>
> April 1, 1996 *(Date)*

Assessment 9
(Lessons 28 - 36)

1. Using a book on your shelf, write a book reference as you would in a bibliography.

2. What is the rhyme scheme of the following hymn?

   Come, Thou Almighty King,
   Help us Thy name to sing,
   Help us to praise;
   Father, all glorious,
   O'er all victorious,
   Come, and reign over us,
   Ancient of Days.
   (Source unknown)

3. Give an example of the following pronouns:

   Singular
   Plural
   Subjective
   Objective
   First person
   Second person
   Third person
   Possessive

4. Use the homonyms *to, too,* and *two* correctly in a sentence.

5. Underline the word *to* in the following sentences. Tell if it is an infinitive or a preposition.

   a. Jack and Jill went to the well.
   b. They wanted to fetch a pail of water.
   c. Jack failed to watch where he was going.
   d. He proceeded to fall down the hill.
   e. Jill went with him to the hospital.

---

1. The general format for a book reference:
   Author's name (last name first). <u>Title</u> (underlined). place of publication: publisher's name in full, copyright date.

2. The rhyme scheme for this hymn is aabcccb.

3. See Personal Pronoun Chart, Lesson 1.
   Examples:
   Singular - I, me, you, he, him, she, her, it
   Plural - we, me, you, them, they
   Subjective - I, you, he, she, we, they
   Objective - me, you, him, her, them, us
   First person - I, me, my
   Second person - you
   Third person - he, him, she, her, they, them
   Possessive - my, mine, your, our, his, her

4. to: a preposition - They are going to the zoo.
   too: also, excessive degree - We are going too.
   two: number - We will need two cars.

5.
   a. Jack and Jill went <u>to</u> the well. (preposition)
   b. They wanted <u>to</u> fetch a pail of water. (infinitive)
   c. Jack failed <u>to</u> watch where he was going. (infinitive)
   d. He proceeded <u>to</u> fall down the hill. (infinitive)
   e. Jill went with him <u>to</u> the hospital. (preposition)

6. *To* is an infinitive when it is followed by a verb. *To* is a preposition when there is a noun following it that answers the question to *whom* or to *what*.

7. William Shakespeare lived in England in 1564-1616.

8. William Shakespeare was an English playwright and poet. He is generally acknowledged to be the greatest dramatist and poet in the English language.

9. malapropism - The writer means "The early rains were a *catastrophe* for the picnic planners.

6. How do you know when *to* is an infinitive? How do you know when *to* is a preposition?

7. When and where did William Shakespeare live?

8. For what is he famous?

9. Read the following sentence:

   The early rains were an apostrophe for the picnic planners.

   This is an example of _____.

Enrichment Answers

The *Enrichment Activities* answers are listed below. Since the *Enrichment Activities* are not numbered, you can easily locate them by the lesson number that proceeds it in the *Student Activity Book*. Some of the *Enrichment Activities* do not have a specific answer. For those, please read the directions in your student's book and evaluate the activity accordingly.

Lesson 1
Words in the puzzle: my   mine   your   yours   her   his   our   their   its

Lesson 2 Answers will vary.

Lesson 3
Down
   1. longest   2. sadder   3. longer
Across
   4. more beautiful   5. oldest   6. older   7. saddest

Lesson 9
A. Possible answers:
   1. dimmer   2. sonnet   3. task   4. articulations   5. aground
   6. shower   7. wagon   8. waited, abated

B. Andrew:hockey   Peter:golf   Stephanie:tennis   Tricia:basketball   Dominic:soccer

C. Answers will vary.

D. Down
      1. cinquain   2. haiku   3. limerick
    Across
      4. diamante   5. simile

E. Answers will vary.

F. 1. mole   molt   bolt   boat
   2. face   fare   fire   firm

Lesson 10
A. Words in the puzzle: is   are   was   were   be   being   been   am

B. Answers will vary.

Lesson 11
1. their   there   2. reel   real   3. would   wood   4. sent   scent   5. hole   whole
6. heir   air

Lesson 12
1. a verb   2. an adjective   3. a noun   4. a noun   5. an adjective

Lesson 15
A. 1. I   2. V   3. E   4. W   5. A   6. X   7. N   8. B   9. J   10. H

B. There she weaves by night and day a magic web with color gay.
   The Lady of Shalott by Lord Alfred Tennyson

C. 1. an adjective   2. a noun   3. a noun   4. an adverb   5. an adjective   6. a verb
   7. an adverb   8. a verb

D. Answers will vary.

Lesson 16   Answers will vary.

Lesson 17
Words in the puzzle: gnaw   reign   sign   sovereign   knock   knot   know   align

Lesson 18
A. 1. race   rice   mice   mine
   2. babe   bale   male   mile

B. Answers will vary.

Lesson 21
A. 1. whale; not land animal
    2. novel; not reference material
    3. Nepal; not South American country
    4. sea; not fresh water
    5. Australia; not northern hemisphere

    6. Mars; not a gaseous planet
    7. William Wordsworth; not painter
    8. Australia; island
    9. F; not formed with curved lines
   10. crow; not a raptor

B. Appliances - oven, microwave, television
    Passive - sleeping, reading, sitting

    Furniture - stool, sofa, table
    Active - running, diving, working

C. 1. body, organ, stomach
    3. universe, galaxy, solar system
    5. professional, doctor, surgeon

    2. man, relative, uncle
    4. animal, mammal, lion
    6. furniture, chair, recliner

D. 1. antonym   2. synonym   3. antonym   4. part/whole   5. category
    6. part/whole   7. characteristic   8. category   9. synonym   10. antonym

E. 1. homonym   2. sequence   3. function   4. degree or sequence   5. function
    6. sequence   7. homonym   8. degree   9. function   10. sequence

F. 1. function   2. degree   3. category   4. antonym   5. homonym
    6. sequence   7. degree   8. category   9. degree   10. sequence
   11. characteristic 12. part/whole   13. function   14. sequence   15. characteristic

Lesson 22
A. 1. dance   2. impious   3. valuable   4. veil   5. edit
    6. season   7. gala   8. border   9. grenade   10. peal

B. 1. hurdle   2. novel   3. defend   4. Monday   5. forget
    6. hilarious   7. engine   8. fail   9. gash   10. perhaps

Lesson 23   Possible answers:
    1. funny   2. college   3. book   4. ecstatic   5. tree
    6. sick   7. pliable   8. knows   9. gas   10. enormous
   11. illuminate   12. piece   13. emotion   14. benefit   15. vehicle
   16. cold   17. yard   18. combustible   19. major league   20. fitness

Lesson 27
A - C. Answers will vary.

D. "I will make you a great nation and bless you and make your name great."
God is speaking to Abraham. It is found in the book of Genesis.

E. Answers will vary.

Lesson 28
Louise:19   Abdul:18   Josh:17   Dan:16   Elliot:14   Rene:13

Lesson 29
And the sea rolled on as it had been rolling for five thousand years. *Moby Dick*

Lesson 32
A. Names found in the puzzle: Dogberry, Don Pedro, Hero, Claudio, Margaret, Antonio, Benedick, Don John, Beatrice, Ursula

B. 1. *As You Like It*   2. *King Lear*   3. *Romeo and Juliet*
   4. *A Midsummer Night's Dream* 5. *Much Ado About Nothing*
   6. *The Merchant of Venice*   7. *Macbeth*   8. *Othello*

C. - D. Answers will vary.

Lesson 36
A. Answers will vary.

B. 1. a conjunction   2. an adjective   3. a preposition   4. a verb
   5. a noun   6. an adverb   7. a conjunction, a verb, a noun
   8. an adjective, an adverb, a preposition

C. - D. Answers will vary.

Skills Index

The numbers listed after each skill refer to the Lesson number.

Book Studies

Star of Light - 13-15
Adam and His Kin - 25-27

Much Ado About Nothing - 30-32

Composition

analogy - A
bibliography - 33
book review - A
character sketch - A
characters - A,19
climax - 19,32
conflict - 19
contrast - A
editing - 9,35,36
first person - A,29
introduction - 19,34
mood - 19
narration - A,C
note-taking - 33
outline - 33,34
paragraph - B,18,34
persuasive writing - A
plot - A,19

poetry - 5-9
point of view - A
prewriting - 19
research - A,C,18
resolution - 19
revising - 9,35
second person - A,29
setting - A,19
supporting sentence - 18
synonym - 12,17
theme - A,19
theme - B
thesis statement - B
third person - A,29
title page - 36
topic - 33
topic sentence - B,18
transitional words - A,B,34

Grammar

Reading

accent - 10
base or root word - 1
cinquain - 6
cliche - 5
climax - C
comedy and tragedy - C
comprehension - A,B,C
diamante - 6
fact - 29
figurative language - 5
haiku - 6
historical fiction - 19
imagery - 5
implied metaphor - 5
internal rhyme - 9
limerick - 6

malapropism - C
memorization - 4-9
metaphor - 5
mood - C
opinion - 29
personification - 5
poetry - 4,9
predicting outcome - A
Psalms - 8
recitation - 4-9
rhyme scheme - 7,28
rhythmic foot - 7,28
simile - 5,28
suffix - 1,2,3,10,16
syllable - 7

Spelling

Add **s** to words ending in **o** - 11
Add suffix **ful** - 2
Add suffix to words ending
    in silent **e** -16,22
Add suffix to words ending in **y**
    - 11,18,23,28
Add suffix to words ending
    with one vowel and one
    consonant - 1,10
ck words - 11
dge words - 1
gh says /**ff**/ - 12

gn / **kn** words - 17
i before **e** rule - 10
ll, ss, ff, zz - 28
Making compound words
    plural and plural
    possessive - 12
tion / **sion** words - 3
ture words - 23
ue / **ew** words - 17
Words with a short vowel and
    double consonants - 29

Study Skills

dictionary - 3,17
encyclopedia - A,C,18,33-35
graphs - B
guide words - 3,17

map skills - A
research - A,B,C,18,33-35
thesaurus - 12

Bibliography

Alcott, Louisa May. *Eight Cousins*. 1874.

Beechick, Ruth. *Adam and His Kin*. Pollock Pines: Arrow Press, 1990.

Chittick, Donald E. *The Controversy—Roots of the Creation Evolution Conflict*. 1984.

Drewery, Mary. *Devil in Print*. 1963.

Lamb, Charles and Mary. *Tales from Shakespeare*. 1807.

Morris, Henry. *The Biblical Basis for Modern Science*. Grand Rapids: Baker Books, 1984.

Morris, Henry. *The Genesis Record*. Grand Rapids: Baker Books.

Norton, Mary. *The Borrowers*. 1952.

Peterson, Dennis R. *Unlocking the Mysteries of Creation*. Sisters: Multnomah Press, 1986.

Sewell, Anna. *Black Beauty*. 1877.

Shakespeare, William. *Much Ado About Nothing*. 1600.

St. John, Patricia. *Star of Light*. Chicago: Moody Press, 1953.